INSTRUCTOR'S GUIDE

CONTEMPORARY'S
NEW BEGINNINGS IN
READING

BONNIE TIVENAN

EDITED BY
DAVID CAES

CONTEMPORARY
BOOKS, INC.
CHICAGO

Contents

Reentry Issues for Adult Learners 1
General Guidelines for Working
   with Adult Beginning Readers 3
New Beginnings in Reading 7
   Placement Test 11
   Sample Lessons 16
      Groundbreaker Exercises 17
      Book 1 28
      Book 2 43
   Extra Features: Pretests, Flash Cards,
   More Reading, Getting Ready, Posttest,
   Certificate of Mastery, Answer Key,
   and Word Lists 57
Suggestions for Teaching Sight Words
   and Phonics 67
Supplemental Materials 69
The Importance of Literacy Work 71
Rationale for New Beginnings in Reading 73
References 77

Consultants
Elaine Belz, M.Ed.
Chad Consuegra, M.S.W.
Rhoda Konigsberg
Susan Paull

The author would like to thank Sandra Stewart, Kate Lindsey, Iris Saltiel, Carrie Weir, and Pat Boos for their help and valuable suggestions. She would also like to acknowledge Lillie May Hadley and Doane Hadley of Attache Business Service, who worked many hours on the word processor.

Editorial Director
Caren Van Slyke

Production Editor
J. D. Fairbanks

Editorial Assistant
Julie Landau

Art and Production
Paul Barnes
Arvid Carlson
Rosemary Morrissey-Herzberg

Typography
David Fultz

Published by Contemporary Books, Inc., 180 North Michigan Avenue, Chicago, Illinois 60601

Published simultaneously in Canada by Beaverbooks, Ltd., 195 Allstate Parkway, Valleywood Business Park, Markham, Ontario L3R 4T8 Canada

Copyright © 1985 by Bonnie Tivenan

All rights reserved. No part of this publication may be reproduced or transmitted in any form or by any means, electronic or mechanical, including photocopy, or any information storage and retrieval system, without permission from the publisher.

ISBN: 0-8092-5166-3

Manufactured in the United States of America

Reentry Issues for Adult Learners

Adult beginning readers seek instruction for numerous reasons. Some hope to obtain a better job. Some want to master the reading process before their children enter school. Some hope to become more independent. Others have been pushed into going back to school by members of their families or concerned friends.

The reasons given by any adult student are very personal. While the reasons for seeking reading instruction vary widely from one student to another, all adult beginning readers have one thing in common—all hope to change themselves and their life situations by learning to read. But even while seeking such a change, it is unlikely that the student is aware of all the changes that becoming literate entails.

Changes in Self-Image

When an adult beginning reader becomes literate, the psychological changes that he may undergo are tremendous. In some ways, the transformation is as drastic as a blind person becoming sighted. The reader will come to perceive his world differently, but even more importantly, he will come to perceive *himself* differently. No longer does the student see himself as a "freak," one of the few who never learned to read, a "failure," or a "powerless victim."

In addition, other people define readers differently than nonreaders. "Less than intelligent" is the common stereotype of the nonreader in our society. The friends and family of the student perceive him differently once he has mastered the reading process. In most instances, a nonreader is seen as a dependent person who must be protected from adult responsibilities, such as banking, paying bills, and applying for jobs. In learning to read, the student declares himself to be independent, capable of adult responsibilities.

Many students are afraid of change. Even though most of these changes seem positive, change is still an extremely difficult process. It is well documented that too much change, even when it is welcomed, causes stress.

For good reason, the student is usually more fearful than even the most nervous bridegroom. A student fears change at the same time that he fears that he will not be able to change. There is the fear that he will not be able to learn how to read. Even though there may be extenuating circumstances which explain why the student did not learn to read the first time around, this fear is really very reasonable. The fact is that the student cannot read, and he cannot read because he had failed at learning to read in the past. Upon reentering the instructional process, the student has no reason to believe that things will be different this time. He only has the hope that change will be possible.

Conflicting Responsibilities

Unfortunately, the student's internal distress is not the only issue that makes reentry into the educational process difficult. Adults frequently carry many responsibilities, some of which may interfere with instruction. It is not uncommon for students to hold two jobs or be involved with an extended family that frequently requires their assistance. Returning to school has to be juggled with these other responsibilities.

Change in Relationships

Frequently, the people that should be the most supportive of the student's reentry into the educational process try to subvert it. Spouses and parents often feel threatened by the changes that accompany literacy. While spouses or parents may consciously want the

---

NOTE: To avoid sexist language, we have alternated male and female pronouns in this book. All references to instructors and students pertain to both sexes except when a specific person is being discussed.

nonreader to become literate, they may also fear that the accompanying changes will drastically alter, if not destroy, their relationship with the adult beginning reader. Consequently, they may unconsciously set up additional stumbling blocks.

Institutional Barriers

It is also important to acknowledge the institutional barriers encountered by the adult beginning reader. Many educational systems are arranged primarily for the convenience of administration, with the staff's needs taking a secondary role and the students' taking last place. Most educational institutions do not provide outreach programs in the areas where they are most needed, so transportation to and from school can become a problem for many students. Similarly, many educational systems do not run day and evening classes, so students who do shift work are excluded from participating in educational programs. In addition, the space allotted to the instruction of beginning readers generally does not allow for privacy. Finally, instructors generally receive very little support in terms of in-service training and budgets for materials.

Summary

While the instructor might feel overwhelmed by the obstacles that must be overcome, it is important to become aware of them. It is through an understanding of these barriers that the instructor will come to appreciate the students' courage and support their dreams and aspirations.

General Guidelines for Working with Adult Beginning Readers

An instructor and an adult student had been assigned to each other for beginning reading instruction. The instructor's initial contact with the student was on the telephone, and they arranged to meet in the local public library at a certain time on a given day. When the instructor arrived at the library at the appointed time, there was only one person in the reading room—a very sophisticated-looking young man, wearing a tie and sports jacket, leafing through a periodical. The instructor walked through the other areas of the library but could not find anyone who fit her student's description. She was about to leave the library when the young man in the sports jacket approached her and identified himself as the person that she was looking for.

You can see that the instructor had made several assumptions about the student that she was about to meet. She had made an assumption about what her student would look like and was surprised that the student looked like one of her peers. Most people who are inexperienced in literacy work do not realize that adult beginning readers are, with one major exception, very much like everyone else.

Inexperienced instructors are frequently influenced by common stereotypes of the adult beginning reader. They are likely to expect that the adult beginning reader will be less intelligent than other people, and they usually think of the adult beginning reader as disadvantaged. What they may fail to realize is that, although the nonreader has not mastered reading, one of the most important skills in our society, she is an adult who is proficient in many other areas. On this basis, the instructor-student relationship should be seen as a partnership of adults.

Characteristics of Adult Beginning Readers

While most experienced instructors will not make the assumptions that the instructor made in the above story, there are certain characteristics that they do expect to see in the adult beginning reader.

While often tentative and embarrassed, the adult nonreader has taken an important step. This involves a great deal of courage on the student's part. Having made this commitment, the student is highly motivated, although she may be plagued by doubts and frustration.

Low Self-Concept

In most instances, an instructor can assume that the adult beginning reader has a poor self-concept, especially as it relates to learning. Most nonreaders feel "dumb" or incompetent because they have not mastered a skill that other people have learned. In most instances, the adult beginning reader feels ashamed and is worried that someone may discover that she has a reading problem. Most adult nonreaders will do whatever they can to prevent others from realizing that they cannot read.

Fear of Failure

Most adult low-level readers have experienced failure in educational settings—long years of failure. Many adult beginning readers do not readily seek reading instruction because they are convinced that they will fail again.

It is important for the instructor to realize that a student fears failure and, at the same time, expects it. This expectation of failure is probably the single

---

NOTE: To avoid sexist language, we have alternated male and female pronouns in this book. All references to instructors and students pertain to both sexes except when a specific person is being discussed.

greatest block to learning. When students believe that they cannot learn, they send themselves "failure messages" that cripple them again and again.

New Beginnings is designed to help break this cycle of failure by providing the student with successful experiences in reading and learning. Small skill increments and large amounts of repetition ensure that the student will succeed. In addition, the content of the material helps students redefine themselves as successful learners. Students who read and comprehend poems, charts, cartoons, maps, and book reviews begin to see themselves as capable of learning.

The Role of the Instructor

While good materials can have a positive impact on the student, it is the instructor's responsibility to use the materials properly. And, while it is important that materials be used properly, the role of the instructor is much broader than that of administrator of materials. The instructor must be sensitive to each student's personal, as well as academic, needs.

Accessibility

Students frequently feel that educators and educational systems have been indifferent to them. In order to offset this negative framework, instructors should be accessible to students. Successful instructors are those that are available to their students, expressing an interest in them as people, not just as students.

Your role as an instructor can go beyond teaching someone how to read. To be most effective, you should express a personal interest in your students—be a friend. Listen to your students when they talk about what is important in their lives. Not only will you be more effective, but you will learn from them. It is important that students realize that both they and the work that they are doing are valued by the instructor.

Patience

Patience is an important attribute of a successful instructor. There will be times when your student will have difficulty learning a skill and times when you do not understand what the problem is. For instance, different people learn to read at different rates. What is easy for one student may be very difficult for another.

Student Progress

The instructor must be patient with the student's progress. Even though a student may not be progressing through the materials as quickly as expected, you can frequently emphasize the progress that the student has already made.

Not only should you emphasize a student's achievements, but you also need to tell the student what her learning strengths are. If a student masters sight words quickly or retains them over a period of time, this should be pointed out as a strength. At the same time, if a student does well with phonics, this should be emphasized. This will help students become realistic in planning their work. For instance, if students know that phonics are difficult for them, then they will be a little more patient with themselves as they work through phonics material.

Responsibility for Learning

If a student expresses doubts about her ability to learn to read, the instructor can decrease the student's anxiety by overemphasizing the instructor's role in the learning process. The instructor can make statements such as "I know that I am a good teacher, and I know that I can help you learn to read." While these statements may take pressure off the student, they are only temporary measures.

As instruction progresses, the instructor has to shift responsibility for learning back to the student. Keeping a log of the student's successes is one way to do this. The log might be as simple as a list of the sight words or skills mastered. If the student's learning rate has improved, notations on time spent per skill should also be included. Since low-level readers frequently feel most comfortable with a regular routine, time for review of the log and the entry of data into it could become a regular part of the student and teacher's time together.

Correcting the Student's Mistakes

You should correct the student's errors in such a way that the student does not feel like a failure. It is best to have students correct themselves.

For example, if a student misreads a word, you can ask the student to reread the sentence to see if the word makes sense. When the student realizes that the word does not make sense, she should be directed to look at the initial consonant and guess what the word is. If the student is able to guess the word correctly, she should repeat the word several times, then reread the sentence.

However, if the student cannot guess the correct word, the instructor should say it for her. The student should look at the word, repeat it several times, and reread the sentence. In both instances, the student-based corrections are followed by a successful experience. Both the instructor and the student can acknowledge that the student had trouble with a word, but it is very important to leave the episode on a positive note.

Diagnosing Student Needs and Abilities

There are many types of methods and materials for diagnosing the student's needs and abilities. *New Beginnings* has a separate *Placement Test* that will help you to place the students at a level that is challenging, but not frustrating. Also, the phonics section of the *Placement Test* will help you to pinpoint both gaps in their knowledge of phonics and materials for remediation.

However, you may encounter some students who have actual physical difficulties with learning to read—vision problems, learning disabilities, etc. This does not mean that they cannot learn to read at all. However, if you suspect that there is a physical difficulty, you may wish to seek the advice of a reading specialist, especially one who has had experience with adults.

Being Honest with the Student

In the previous sections, we have talked about how the instructor's actions can affect the student's success. But you can directly affect the student's success in many indirect ways. By showing that you take the student's work seriously, you can boost her self-confidence and motivate her to try even harder. Be enthusiastic about the student's progress, but be realistic and honest as well. Don't set overly high expectations for the student and don't give praise when it isn't due. If the student senses that your compliments are false, she will become suspicious.

SETTING REALISTIC GOALS

Being honest with a student includes helping the student set realistic goals. Setting appropriate goals does not mean that the instructor should tear apart a student's goals as impractical or impossible, but it does mean that you should be able to suggest realistic alternatives. For example, if a thirty-year-old beginning reader who works as a laborer expresses interest in health care, the instructor might suggest that there are numerous positions in the hospital that provide rewarding career opportunities. The instructor can also broaden the student's awareness of job opportunities by helping her to identify the characteristics that attract her to a particular type of job. Then, the instructor can help her identify similar jobs.

Setting short-range goals is also a useful strategy to encourage students and help them to learn how to set realistic goals. Short-range goals can be set according to what the instructor plans to cover during a month or over several months. If the student is working exclusively in *New Beginnings*, goals can be set according to the skills and vocabulary words that will be covered during a time interval or in terms of the number of lessons that will be completed.

CONFRONTING DEFEATIST ATTITUDES

Being honest with the students includes making them aware of their defeatist attitudes. Many students approach a new task with an expectation of failure. This affects their attendance and completion of assignments. This expectation of failure is frequently to blame when absences and incomplete assignments are followed by weak excuses such as "I missed the bus" or "I was too upset to do my homework or to come to school." By challenging the student's defeatist attitude in a gentle but firm manner, the instructor can confront the student's assumption that she can't learn.

BEING SUPPORTIVE OF THE STUDENT

Creating an atmosphere in which adult students feel comfortable sharing their feelings is not an easy task, yet it is an important goal. Student who feel free to talk about why they never learned to read have a chance to develop insights that will free them to learn.

The instructor can support this process by directing the student to look beyond the superficial. For example, perhaps a student just remembers that she "didn't like school." Trying to get the student to identify a particular feeling or cause (e.g., an indifferent teacher) might help her to see that there were reasons she didn't learn to read, reasons that were beyond her control when she was a child.

Summary

These guidelines suggest that the instructor must recognize the emotional as well as the intellectual components of learning. To this end, the instructor must be sensitive, gentle, tough, honest, structured, flexible, and insightful. Indeed, the list could be extended to such an extent that no one would or could attempt the task. However, one final suggestion makes the task less threatening.

It is strongly suggested that the instructor provide a framework in which the student takes responsibility for her own education. Since many students are initially not able to assume this responsibility, the shift of responsibility from the instructor to the student will need to be gradual. Yet, from the very first meeting, you can share responsibility with the student. You can begin by outlining the sequence of skills to be mastered. Before each lesson, you can explain what will be covered during the lesson and why it is important.

As instruction proceeds, you can share your observations on the student's learning style and can solicit the student's opinion on the materials used and the teaching techniques employed. Finally, you can act as an adviser to the student who has begun to set her own goals.

New Beginnings in Reading

Overview

New Beginnings in Reading provides high-quality instruction for adult and adolescent beginning readers. It readily lends itself to use with students who are low-level readers and is designed to bring students up to a third-grade reading level. The nine books in the series may also be used to reinforce the reading skills of students who are reading at the third- or fourth-grade reading level.

The instruction in *New Beginnings in Reading* is presented in small skill increments, with large amounts of repetition. Each book builds on the skills and sight words presented in the earlier books. Adult-oriented material is heavily emphasized throughout the series.

New Beginnings utilizes an eclectic approach to reading. It uses a sight word approach, with only seven new words introduced in each lesson, but it also emphasizes phonics (a sound-symbol approach) as well as the use of context (using familiar words to figure out unfamiliar words). The combination of these techniques will help the student become an effective reader.

Assumptions About Beginning Readers

New Beginnings does make several assumptions about a student's abilities. *New Beginnings* assumes that the student can recognize the word as a unit in reading. It assumes that the student knows that reading progresses from the left to right and flows down a page. And finally, it assumes that the student can either print or write the letters of the alphabet, although the student does not have to know the sounds made by the letters.

While failure to meet all of these assumptions may temporarily postpone a student's entry into *New Beginnings*, some of these skills can be developed while the student is working through the material in the program. You will find several suggestions for working with extremely low-level students in the paragraphs below.

1. If the student needs to learn to recognize the word as a unit, this can best be accomplished by teaching the student his own name and other words that he finds meaningful. For example, an expectant mother may want to learn to read the words *baby*, *diapers*, *labor*, and *midwife*. These words can be combined into sentences to illustrate that readers of English read from left to right and pause to recognize meaning at periods.

2. If the student cannot print or write the letters of the alphabet, he can still begin work in *New Beginnings* while simultaneously working on writing skills. During the interval in which the student is learning to write, he can dictate to the instructor any exercise that requires writing. As the student becomes more proficient, the instructor should write the exercise on a separate piece of paper and then have the student copy it into the book.

Approaches to Beginning Reading

New Beginnings in Reading is appropriate for low-level readers because it makes few assumptions about a student's reading skills. The books are developed with small skill increments and large amounts of repetition that result in the student's mastery of the reading process.

SIGHT WORDS: Starting in Lesson 1 of each book, only seven sight words are introduced per lesson. The

---

NOTE: To avoid sexist language, we have alternated male and female pronouns in this book. All references to instructors and students pertain to both sexes except when a specific person is being discussed.

sight words are meaningful to adults and useful in readings with adult topics. The pages that follow contain readings and exercises that reinforce those words. Each lesson that follows adds only seven new sight words and builds on the words presented in previous lessons. Each sight word is generally used at least ten times in the lesson in which it is introduced.

PHONICS: *New Beginnings* provides for student success in other ways too. Only one phonics principle is introduced in any given book, and those skills are reviewed in the books that follow.

The phonics principles are used to form word families. For instance, with the short **a** sound, students learn the "at" words: *fat, hat, mat, sat,* etc. This reinforces the phonics skills and builds the students' vocabularies.

SUFFIXES AND PREFIXES: Suffixes or prefixes are taught in each book—no more than two per book. The prefix or suffix is repeated throughout the book in which it is introduced.

Adult Orientation of Materials

To become a successful reader, the adult student needs more than small skill increments, large amounts of repetition, and familiarity with different reading techniques. *New Beginnings* is designed to give the student a successful learning experience so that the student will come to perceive himself as capable of mastering the reading process. In part, *New Beginnings* attempts to instill this confidence through adult-oriented material. The material is aimed specifically at an adolescent and adult audience so that the student is not humiliated by children's texts and is highly motivated by adult topics and issues.

The Components of New Beginnings

New Beginnings in Reading has four major components:
1. *The Placement Test*—geared to starting students at *Groundbreaker Exercises, Book 3,* or *Book 6*
2. *Groundbreaker Exercises*—a slow-paced introductory text
3. *Books 1-8*—the main texts
4. *Instructor's Guide*

Placement Test

The *Placement Test*, which is used to place the student in the proper book in the series, is divided into a word list, three reading sections, and a phonics section.

WORD LIST

The word list is simply a list of ten words that is used to screen out students who would be frustrated by the *Placement Test*. If a student cannot read at least 8 of these words, then the remaining sections of the *Placement Test* would prove to be too frustrating for the student.

READINGS

The *Placement Test* contains three readings. The first reading contains comments by three adults on what reading means to them. The second reading is a personal account of how one man initiated his own exercise program. The third reading is about the consequences of being laid off.

PHONICS

Whereas the other sections of the *Placement Test* are designed to place a student in a particular book in *New Beginnings*, the phonics sections of the *Placement Test* are designed to assess a student's phonics abilities. The test is divided into five sections, each designed to test a different skill.

When the student has completed the phonics section of the *Placement Test*, the instructor should have a good idea of the phonics skills that the student needs help with.

For example, if the phonics sections shows that the student knows the consonant sounds but does not know the short vowel sounds, then the instructor should plan on spending more time on the short vowel sounds and relatively little time on the consonant sounds. Similarly, if the student knows the "s" and "t" sounds but cannot identify the "j" or "h," then the instruction should focus on the "j" and "h" sounds, with relatively little time being spent on those sounds that the student already knows.

A chart that shows where the series focuses on different vowel and consonant sounds can be found on page 68.

By using the information from the *Placement Test*, the instructor will be able to tailor a curriculum to an individual student's needs. This will focus on those areas in which the student needs help and will not waste time on those areas in which the student does not. Experience has shown that students are particularly responsive to this strategy.

Groundbreaker Exercises

New Beginnings—Groundbreaker Exercises is an introductory book in this series. It assumes that the student has no reading vocabulary.

Even though the first lesson of *Groundbreaker Exercises* uses only seven words, all exercises and activities in that lesson and the subsequent six lessons are based on higher-level thinking skills. Since this series is oriented toward adults and not children, the material reflects an adult's intellectual maturity.

Books 1-8

The adult content continues throughout the higher-level books of *New Beginnings*. The material in the different books reflects different orientations.

ODD BOOKS

The odd-numbered books (1, 3, 5, 7) are geared to a life-skills orientation with adult issues. Each of the odd books has a similar organization. The theme of Lesson 1 in the odd books is health. The theme of Lesson 2 is consumer economics. Lesson 3 is concerned with employment. Lesson 4 emphasizes housing, and Lesson 5 concentrates on the government.

EVEN BOOKS

Each of the even-numbered books (2, 4, 6, 8) also has a similar organization, focusing on reading. In the even books, Lesson 1 contains facts related to literacy. Lesson 2 provides a biographical sketch of a famous person who did not learn to read until he or she was older. In Lesson 3, there are book reviews of books on learning to read. Lesson 4 highlights a famous person who had a form of learning disability. Lesson 5 contains the accounts of several adult beginning readers. They talk about why they never learned to read, why they are now back in school, how they feel about learning to read, and, in Book 8, what they are going to do in the future.

Special Features

Comprehension and Open-Ended Questions

In addition to providing high-interest materials, *New Beginnings* includes several other features. Even in the earliest exercises, *New Beginnings* provides several different types of comprehension activities.

New Beginnings contains literal comprehension questions that can be used to see if the student understands the details in what he is reading. In addition to these, there are inference questions, most of which are open-ended. They are structured so the student must explain his reasons for a specific choice and not simply respond with a "right" or "wrong" answer. Similarly, values clarification activities and word association activities are personal responses and cannot be marked "right" or "wrong".

QUIZZES IN ODD BOOKS

The odd and even books contain different types of quizzes. The quiz in the odd books focuses on the theme of that lesson and makes several statements that can be answered by circling yes or no. The answers that are provided show what other adults think about this question. It is not anticipated that the students will know all of the answers to these questions, but it will show the student how others view the same issues. The quiz should be treated as a high-interest activity. There are not necessarily any "right" or "wrong" answers in these activities.

QUIZZES IN EVEN BOOKS

Most of the quizzes in the even-numbered books are based on the facts already presented in that lesson. Two of the exercise types require literal comprehension skills. Answers to these quiz questions can be found at the back of the book. These quizzes also include two exercises that contain inferential questions, asking the students what they think about an issue.

Spelling and Writing Activities

New Beginnings provides other activities that can motivate the student and reinforce reading.

SPELLING

Many students express a strong interest in learning how to spell. Following the word families exercises at the end of each "Sounding It Out," there is a section devoted to spelling. The instructor should use the student's skill as a guideline in conducting this exercise. For students who are not that interested in spelling, this activity can be used as an exercise in which the instructor says the word and the student finds it and copies it. For students who are more interested in spelling, it can be conducted more rigorously, as a spelling test.

WRITING

"Time to Write" is a language-experience activity that serves as a high motivation for many students and reinforces the reading process. The structured writing activity is a feature in every lesson in *New Beginnings*. Models are provided so that the student can see what others have written. The instructor should assist the student in spelling any words that he has difficulty with.

If the student seems uncomfortable writing, he can dictate the writing exercise to the instructor. The instructor should write it on a separate piece of paper and then let the student copy it into the book, after getting the student's approval. The instructor should use the student's level of ability as a guideline as to how to conduct the exercise.

Tips on How To Improve Your Reading

One of the unusual features in *New Beginnings* is the "Tips on How to Improve Your Reading," which are read by the instructor. The tips are presented in every lesson of this series and provide useful information about the reading process. A sample of the issues in the tips includes the importance of conditioning oneself to relax while reading, suggestions on how to learn difficult words, and suggestions on how to schedule reading time at home. While the tips are to be read by the instructor to the student, it is recommended that the instructor and the student discuss them. The instructor and the student can evaluate the tips and plan for their implementation.

Answer Keys

Although many of the questions are open-ended, and there are no correct answers, a good number of the questions in *New Beginnings* are comprehension questions that have correct answers. The directions at the bottom of the pages indicate which pages have the answers.

The answer key is at the end of each book. Some students may enjoy correcting their own work.

Practical Tools for Implementation

Since *New Beginnings in Reading* was written by a reading specialist who had experience in a classroom setting, in a learning center, and in one-to-one tutorial sessions, the series has been designed to be practical.

The material in *New Beginnings* is flexible enough to be used in either a small-group setting or a one-to-one tutorial. After students become comfortable with the exercise types in *New Beginnings*, they can do several of the activities in each lesson without assistance so that the instructor can assist other students.

A **pretest** begins each book, so that if the separate placement test is not available, the instructor can use the pretest to determine whether or not a particular book is appropriate for the student. Similarly, a word list at the end of each book can be used for placing students who are resistant to testing.

Flash cards are available at the back of each book for all of the sight words in that book. The flash cards have the sight word on one side and a sentence with the sight word on the back. For many of the words, there are picture clues.

"More Reading" provides the student with four or five pages of additional, independent reading in *Books 2–8*. These readings follow the lives of Dan and Jane.

A **posttest** assists the instructor in determining whether or not a particular student is ready for the next book in *New Beginnings*. A **certificate of mastery** is included in each book to help celebrate the student's completion of that book.

Most importantly, the series was designed to be practical in terms of time management. Independent work is interspersed throughout the lessons, in the pages with **"On Your Own"** at the top. Even in *Groundbreaker Exercises*, independent work was included so that the instructor could, if necessary, work with several students who are working at different levels. This also gives the student an opportunity to work independently.

Finally, the **overview** on the back cover of each book summarizes, in a chart, the range of word attack skills in the entire series. This provides a quick reference to the phonics skills, prefixes or suffixes, and sight words in each book.

Placement Test

The following sample pages illustrate key features from the *Placement Test*, a separate book in the *New Beginnings* series. It can be used to diagnose phonetic weaknesses and to place students in *Groundbreaker Exercises*, *Book 3*, or *Book 6*.

The *Placement Test* contains a word list, three reading sections, a phonics section, a complete set of directions for the instructor, and a flow chart that presents an overview of how the student should progress through the *Placement Test*.

The *Placement Test* begins by presenting ten words in isolation. The word list is intended to act as a screening device so that students who would be frustrated by the reading section of the *Placement Test* can be placed immediately in *Groundbreaker Exercises*. The words that have been chosen are from the first reading section.

The directions and flow chart for administering the *Placement Test* can be found at the back of the test.

The instructor should read the instructions to the student and allow about five to seven seconds to say the word before providing it for the student.

Avoid using the word "test", as some students are frightened by testing. The instructor should explain to the student that this is a very brief and useful booklet for placing the student into the correct book in *New Beginnings*.

The directions at the bottom of this page indicate that the instructor should read the instructions to the student.

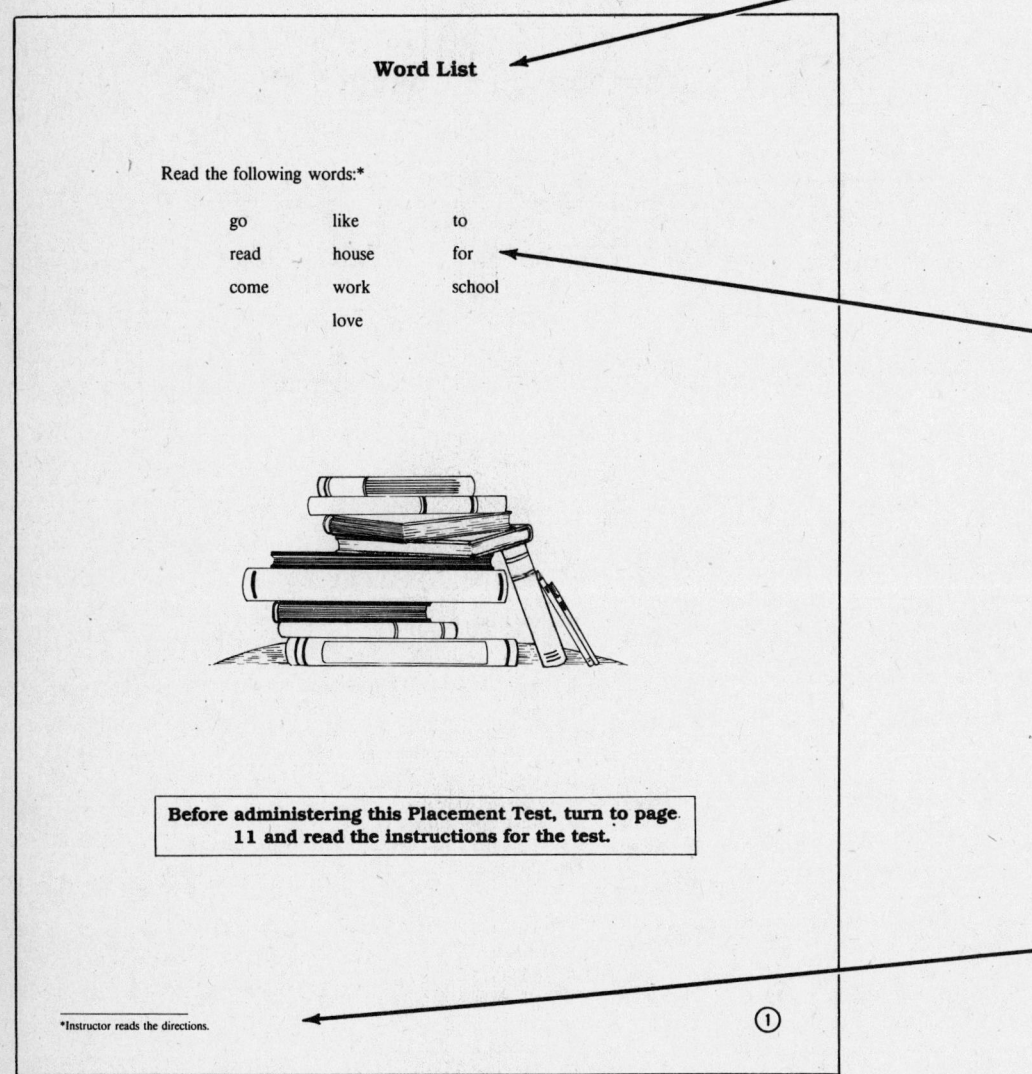

Reading Section 2 is representative of the three readings on the *Placement Test*. In each section, the student is asked to read a story aloud. In the second and third readings, the instructor and student should discuss the questions that follow the readings.

During the administration of this placement test, feel free to stop to talk about the topic of the reading. This may be your first encounter with the student. Spend time getting to know the student, and let him get to know you.

As the student reads each section, the instructor should discreetly note any words that she has difficulty with. If a student makes the same error more than once, this should only be recorded as one error, as it is a repeat of a previous error.

The directions and flow chart on pages 11–13 of the *Placement Test* note that if a student cannot identify six or more words in this passage, he should complete levels 1 and 2 of the **Phonics Test** and begin work with *Book 3* of New Beginnings.

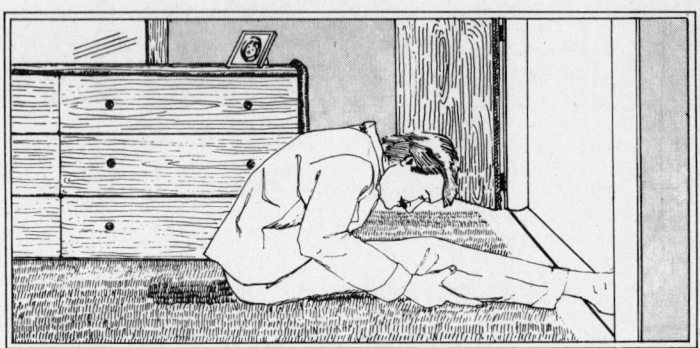

SECTION 2

How Exercise Changed My Life

by Rick Long

I used to have a weight problem. I am not kidding. I have a sales job. I don't get any exercise at work. And I did not exercise on my own. I like to read the newspaper. So sometimes I would pick up a paper. But that was all the exercise I got! And I used to eat sweets all day.

Again and again friends told me that I had to change my ways. I knew that they were trying to help me. But I was not interested. I just was not ready. I invented 100 ways to get out of exercising. Then one day I got locked out of my house. I could not fit through a window to get back in. I saw what was happening to me. And I did not like it. Right then and there I decided to change my life.

I have done just that. I have changed in 2 big ways. I no longer eat things that have a lot of calories. And I have been exercising 2 hours a day. When I get up, I do 100 sit-ups. Then I am out on the city streets jogging before it is even light.

> I have been exercising for 2 years now. And I will not kid you. Sometimes exercising is hard. Most of the time it is lonely. But sometimes it is fun. I work out with friends 1 or 2 nights and we always have a good time.
>
> Exercise is good in other ways too. Many people have told me that I look much younger. I feel different. Now my clothes fit right. And I feel safer too. I am very happy about losing weight. But sometimes I don't believe it. I have gone through a lot. But sometimes I think that I still have a weight problem.
>
> ──────── **Things to Think About*** ────────
>
> What do you think of people who exercise 2 hours a day?
>
> Could you exercise for 2 hours a day? Do you have the time?
>
> Do you want to exercise for 2 hours a day?
>
> Why does Rick still think that he has a weight problem?
>
> ⑤
>
> *These can be the focus for discussion after reading the passage.

If the student experiences difficulty reading the passage, tell him that you would like to complete the reading. Reassure him that after completing *Book 5* in *New Beginnings* she will be able to read **Section 2**.

Either the student or the instructor can read the comprehension questions. These can serve as the basis for a discussion about what has just been read.

The directions at the bottom of the page give general guidelines. More complete instructions can be found on pages 11–13 of the *Placement Test*.

14 NEW BEGINNINGS IN READING: INSTRUCTOR'S GUIDE

The **Phonics Test** has five sections. The directions and flow chart indicate which levels of the **Phonics Test** should be done. It is suggested that the instructor have a separate copy of the test to note how the student mispronounces various letters and sounds.

When working on each section of the **Phonics Test**, concentrate on the sound being presented in that particular section. For example, if a student is working on Level 2, focus on how the student pronounces the short vowel sounds.

Level 1 tests the consonant sounds **a** and **i**.

Level 1 tests the consonant sounds.

Level 2 tests the short vowels sounds for **a** and **i** by directing the student to read six nonsense syllables.

Nonsense syllables are used to focus on the student's recognition of a particular sound.

Level 3 tests the short vowels sounds for **e**, **o**, and **u** by directing the student to read nine nonsense syllables.

Instructions at the bottom of the page note that the directions should be read to the student by the instructor.

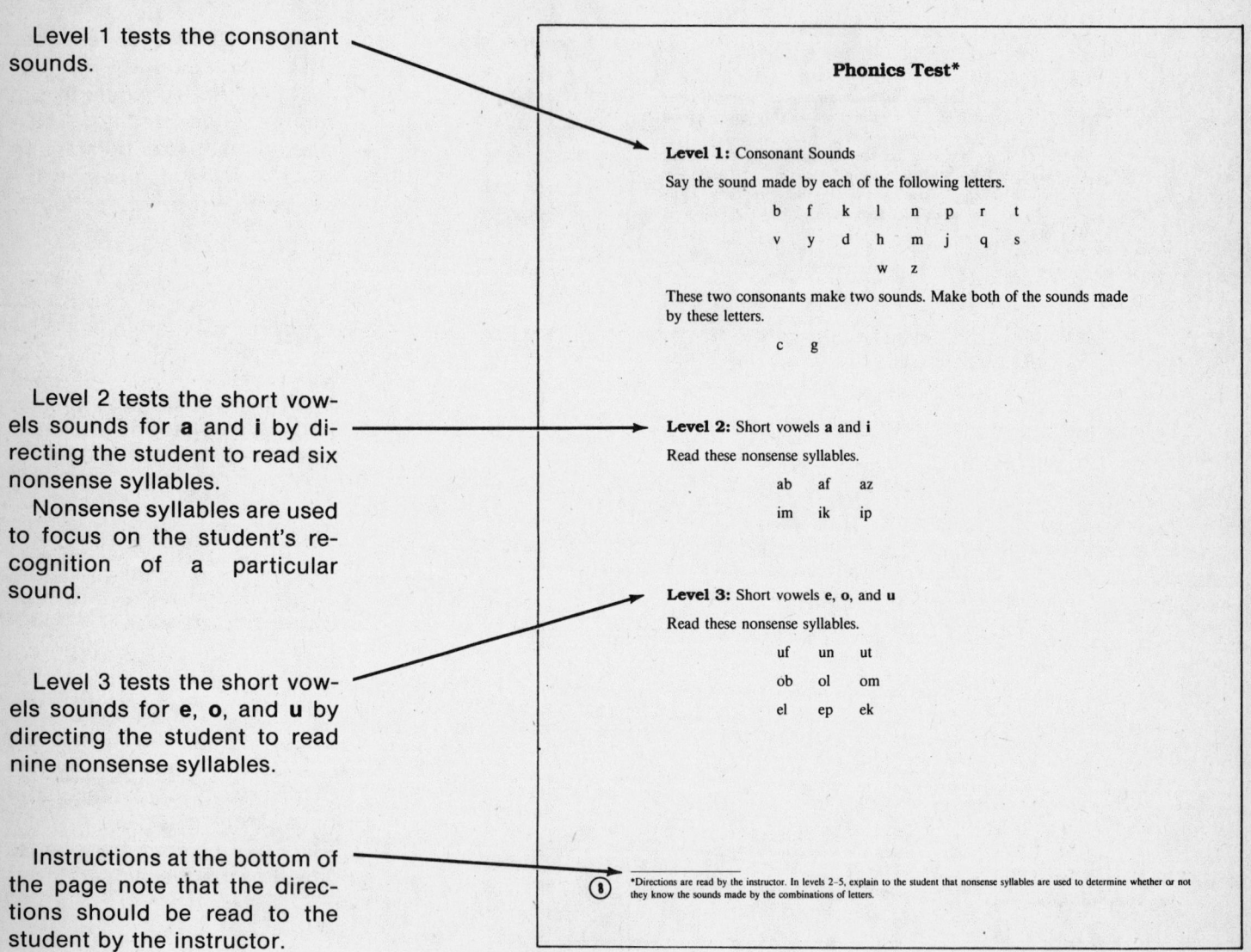

Placement Test 15

Level 4: Long Vowels
Read these nonsense syllables.

<pre>
ake   ope   ine   ule   eal
eet   oap   ain   ay   ite
</pre>

Level 4 tests all the long vowels (vowels that say themselves) by directing the student to read ten nonsense syllables.

Level 5: Consonant Blends and Digraphs
Read these nonsense syllables.

<pre>
blap   clet   flet   glod   plu
bren   cril   drat   frug   graz
whik   thof   chug   chen   shib
slan   pren   shof   tra
</pre>

Level 5 uses nonsense words to test consonant blends and digraphs. (The "consonant digraphs" are "sh," "ch," "th," and "wh." All of the other combinations are consonant blends.)

The **Phonics Test** relies on nonsense syllables to test the student's knowledge of the sounds so that the student cannot use her knowledge of words as a cue.

Levels 1-5 of the **Phonics Test** represent all the phonics principles taught in *New Beginnings in Reading*.

Sample Lessons

It is important that the instructor be aware of some of the features found in the lessons in *New Beginnings* and know how to use the various exercises.

Sample lessons have been developed for three books: *Groundbreaker Exercises*, *Book 1*, and *Book 2*. Each sample lesson will show the exercise, describe what it is, and illustrate how it is to be used. In many places, there are also suggestions for alternative exercises if the student has difficulty with an exercise or needs to do additional work with a particular skill.

Sample lessons are included for *Groundbreaker Exercises* because it is the introductory book in *New Beginnings*—probably the most important book in the series. It is the first book that many students will use, so it is important that the instructor also know how to use it.

As you may recall from earlier sections in the *Instructor's Guide*, the odd and even books have different orientations. Sample lessons are included for *Book 1* and *Book 2* because they represent the patterns followed in the odd and even books.

Why aren't sample lessons included for all of the books? The organization of the later books in the series is very similar to that of *Book 1* and *Book 2*, with many of the same exercise types carried throughout all of the books. Besides, by the time you get to the later books, you are going to be an "old hand" at using *New Beginnings* and will not need the sample lessons!

NOTE: To avoid sexist language, we have alternated male and female pronouns in this book. All references to instructors and students pertain to both sexes except when a specific person is being discussed.

GROUNDBREAKER EXERCISES
Lesson 2

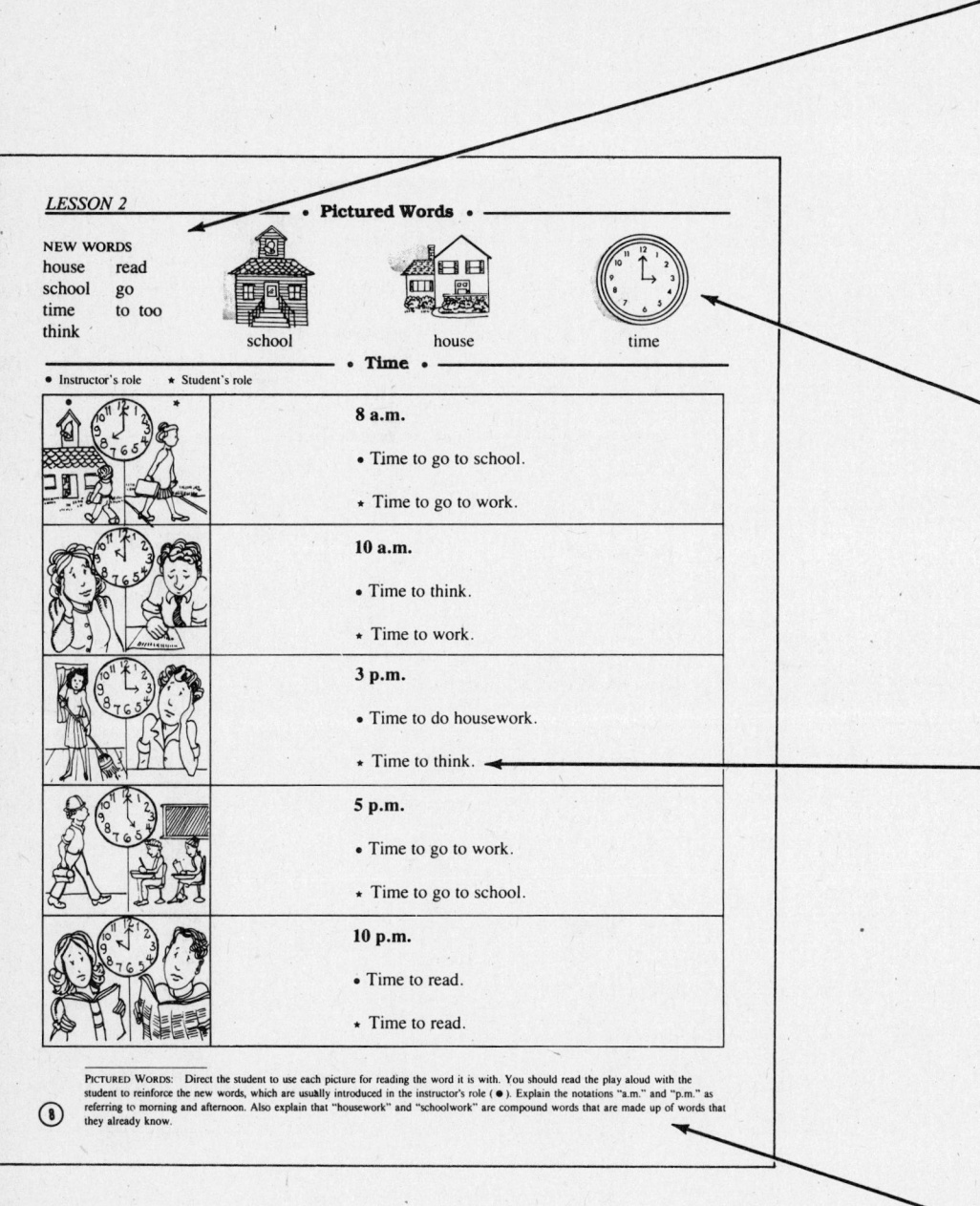

In *Groundbreaker Exercises*, new words are always found in the upper left-hand corner of the page. Introducing new words should be the first activity of the lesson. The instructor should read each word and have the student repeat the word while looking at it. This activity should be repeated several times before proceeding to the next activity, **Pictured Words**.

Pictures are included as cues for some of the new words. If a student has difficulty remembering a word, he can then use the pictures as a clue.

In *Groundbreaker Exercises*, a **play** is used to reinforce the new words. The instructor's role (●) always comes first. The dot (●) and the star (★) in the first frame show what characters are being portrayed. In Lesson 2, the dot and the star indicate that the instructor portrays the person on the left side of the frame and the student reads the part of the person on the right. In order to provide the student with additional practice with the new words, the play can be repeated several times and the roles reversed.

Directions on the bottom of the page explain how to use the page. The directions also explain any special features of the page.

Dots on either side of the title indicate that this activity is instructor-assisted.

The crossword puzzle reinforces the new words. The student looks at the picture clues, which are taken directly from the **Pictured Words**, and then writes those words. The student may copy the spelling of each word from the pictured words. The initial letter for each word in the crossword puzzle is provided so that the student will not have difficulty with the placement of the word.

In "**What Do You Think?**" the student looks at a picture, reads the two sentences under it, and then decides which sentence better describes the picture. Although the directions specify that the student should write the best sentence on the line, if the student is learning to write or appears frustrated, the correct number of the sentence can be put on the line.

The directions at the bottom of the page show the instructor how to use that page. They also give the answer key page number for the exercises that have answers.

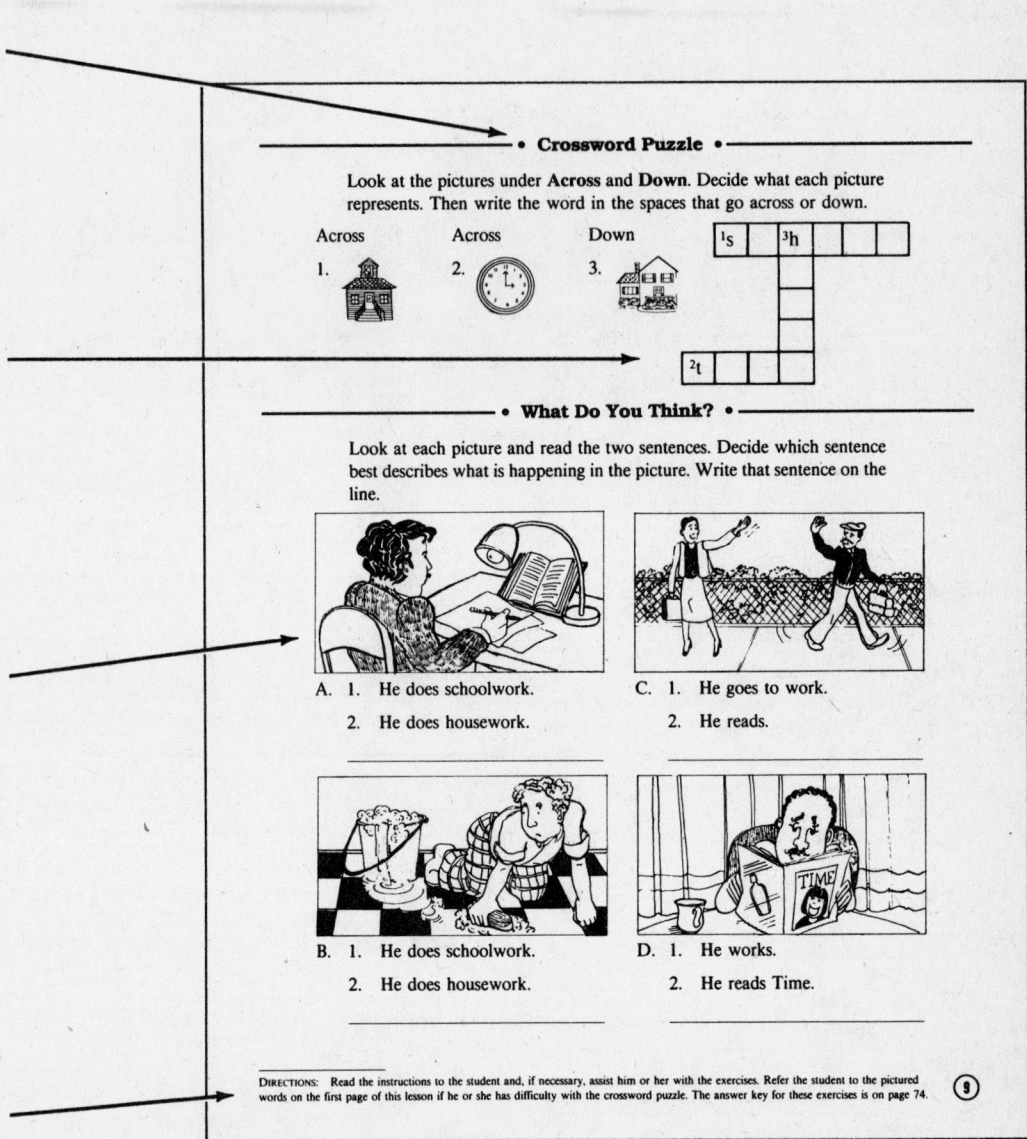

Sample Lessons—Groundbreaker Exercises 19

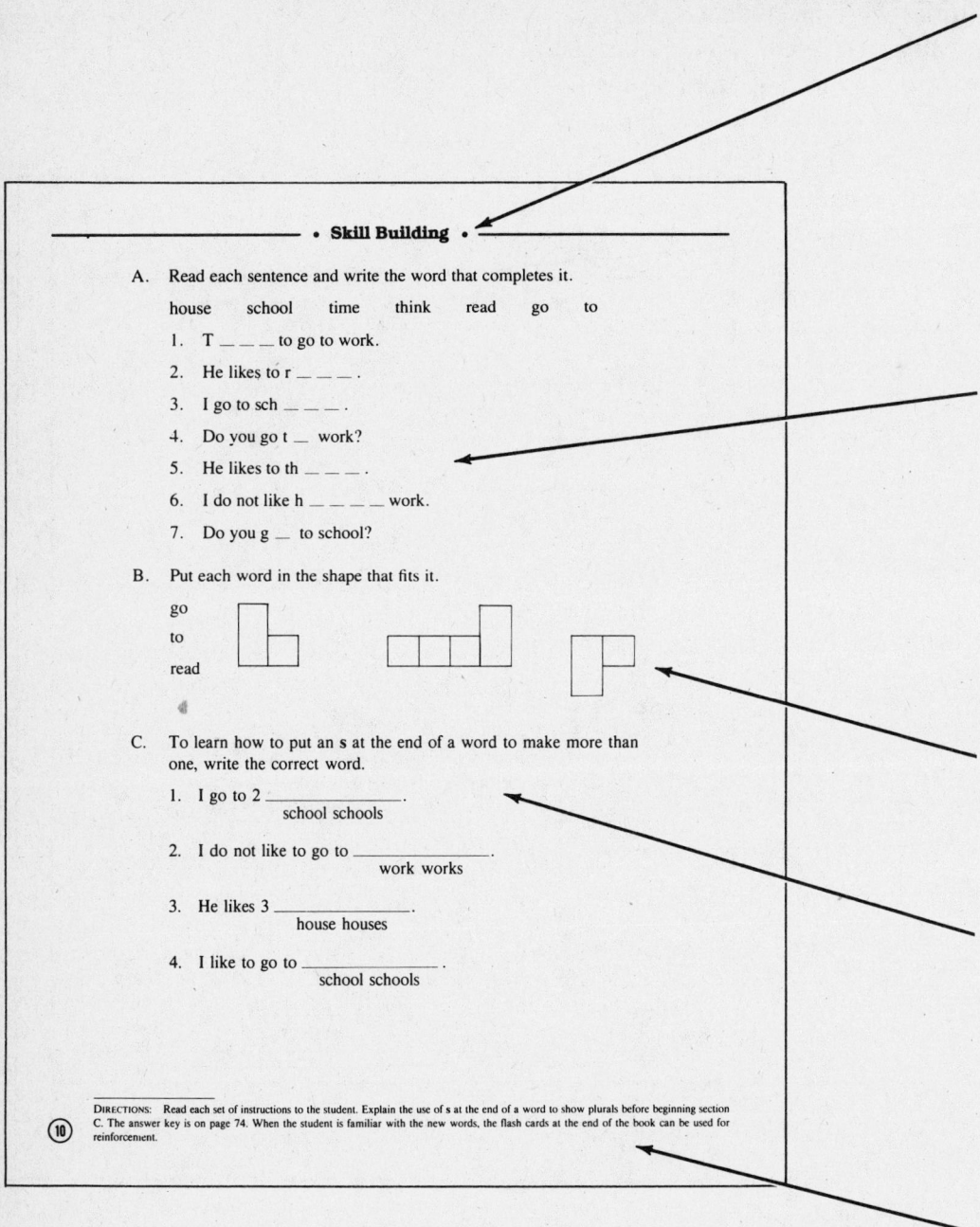

Skill Building is instructor-assisted, as indicated by the dots. **Skill Building** gives the student an opportunity to review old skills and develop new ones.

The student is asked to use the meaning of each sentence to determine which word goes in the blank. This exercise uses all of the new words from this lesson so that the student has a chance to practice with these new vocabulary words.

Learning how to use the meaning of a sentence to determine an unfamiliar word is very useful for beginning readers. Using sentence meaning is one of the basic methods that a reader applies to figure out an unfamiliar word.

Students are asked to look at the shape of a word and then write it in the correct set of boxes. This can serve as a memory aid for many beginning readers.

The **-s** ending is taught by asking the student to select the correct word for each sentence. This gives the student another tool for working with unknown words.

The directions at the bottom of the page explain how this page is to be used. This particular set of directions contains a reminder that only the plural **-s** ending is taught in this lesson.

There is also a note about where the answer key and flash cards can be found.

It is strongly suggested that the **"On Your Own"** activities be assigned for independent work. While students should be encouraged to do the activities on their own, the instructor may want to follow up these activities by discussing the stories with the student.

The **"On Your Own"** activities vary from book to book, but the lessons within each book follow a similar format from lesson to lesson.

Stars (★) are used throughout *New Beginnings* to indicate exercises that the student should be encouraged to do on his own.

The word find reinforces the new words from each lesson by presenting them in a sentence and then in the word find. This is usually one of the most popular activities in each lesson, as it provides a successful experience for each student.

In *Groundbreaker Exercises*, "**Read, Read, Read**" has two comic strips for the student to read and enjoy, some of which are quite humorous. This shows the student that reading can be an enjoyable activity.

The directions give general guidelines on the use of this page and indicate that "**On Your Own**" can be assigned as independent work when the student is familiar with the format.

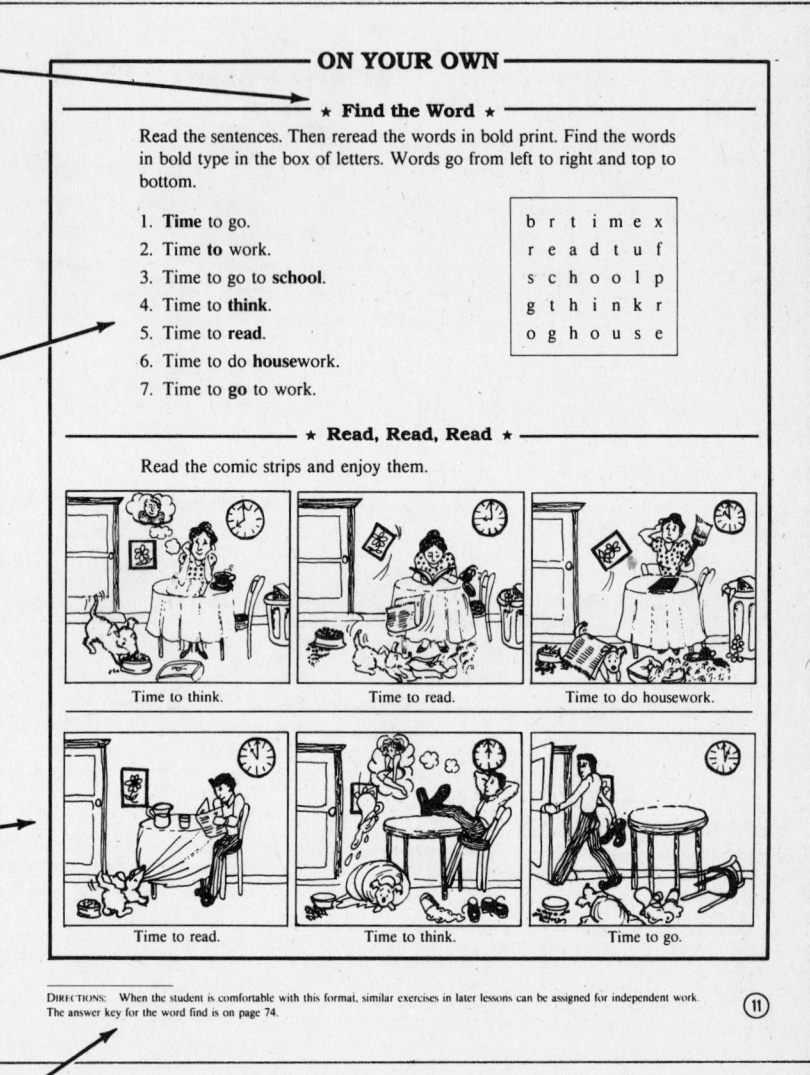

Sample Lessons—Groundbreaker Exercises   21

"**On Your Own**" activities should be assigned as independent work as soon as the student is capable of doing the exercises on his own.

In "**Make Your Own Comic**," the student is given the first picture in a series and is asked to place the second and third pictures in the proper order. Placing a series of events in sequence is a skill that is useful in improving reading comprehension as it will help the reader order events in time or space sequence.

ON YOUR OWN

★ Make Your Own Comic Strip ★

The first part of the comic strip is numbered **1**. Look at the other 2 parts and decide which part comes next. Put a **2** on the part that comes second and a **3** on the part that comes third.

1. He goes to work.

★ Playing with Words ★

Unscramble the following sentences.

Example: read to like I.   I like to read.

1. go You school to.   You go _____.
2. not He think does.   He does _____.
3. like I school.   I _____.
4. you Do school like?   Do _____?
5. I housework do.   I _____.

★ How Are You Doing? ★

In this lesson you have answered 35 questions. Count the number of questions you got wrong and look at the chart to see how you did.

NUMBER WRONG	0–3	Excellent	NUMBER WRONG	10–12	Good
	4–6	Great		13–15	OK
	7–9	Very good			

⑫ DIRECTIONS: When the student is comfortable with this format, similar exercises in later lessons can be assigned for independent work. The instructor will need to assist the student with the words in "How Are You Doing?" The answer key is on page 74.

The student is directed to put the scrambled words into a sequence that forms a sentence. If a student experiences difficulty, it is suggested that the instructor place all but two or three of the words into their proper sequence. As the student works through *New Beginnings*, the instructor should give less and less assistance with this type of exercise, until the student can do it without assistance.

The student is given the opportunity to evaluate his performance in this lesson. The instructor should remember that students need a large amount of positive reinforcement, even if the student's performance was less than perfect. Emphasize the ways that the student is improving as a reader.

Directions at the bottom of the page suggest that the activities in "**On Your Own**" can be assigned as independent work as soon as the student is able to handle them alone.

Dots around the title indicate that **"Time to Write"** is an instructor-assisted activity.

"Time to Write" is a structured language-experience activity. First the student reads material that others have written. In this lesson, two people have written their daily schedules. The student is then asked to write his schedule.

In the **"Time to Write"** exercises, the instructor should assist the students with spelling any words that they need help with. If the student has difficulty generating ideas, the student may copy one of the models word for word. If the student has difficulty writing, he may dictate his thoughts to the instructor. The instructor should write the student's thoughts on a separate piece of paper and then let the student copy it into the book. Students who dictate their writings should be encouraged to begin writing their own compositions as they move through later books in *New Beginnings*.

The directions at the bottom of the page give the instructor suggestions on how to present this activity to the student.

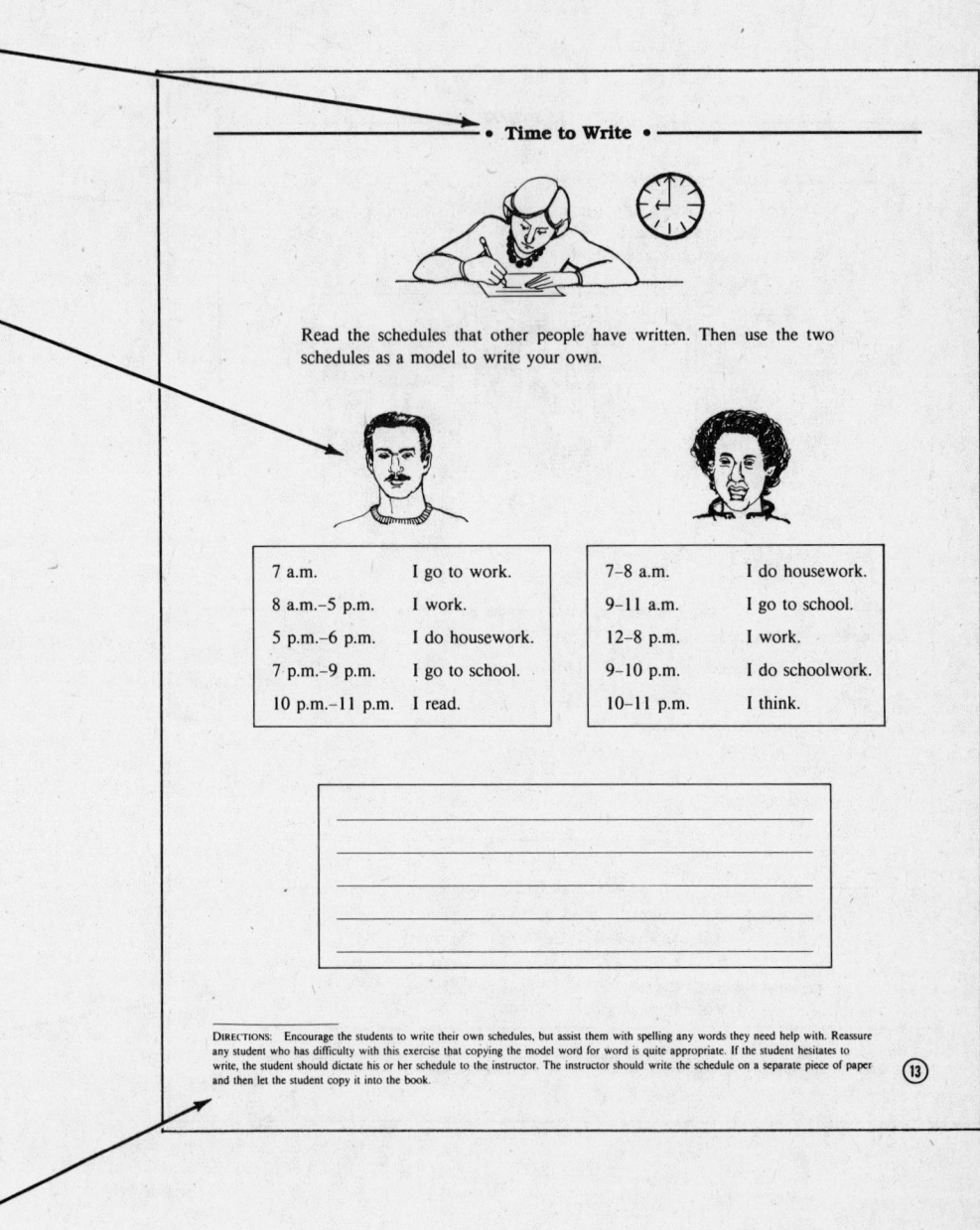

• Tips on How to Improve Your Reading •
(To be read to the student by the instructor)

In Lesson 1 we talked about why it is important to learn the sounds that the letters make. Now we will look at some ways of learning the sounds.

One very good way to learn a sound is through a *guide word*. A guide word is a word that helps you remember a sound. Here is an example. *Man* can be used as a guide word for **m**. If you have trouble remembering the **m** sound, you can think of the word *man*. As you say *man* to yourself, you can hear the **m** sound. Then you can say the **m** sound.

Choosing the right guide word is very important. Some words will be easier for you to remember than others. If your wife's name is Mary, you could use *Mary* as a guide word. Words that you can picture in your mind are also good. *Map* or *magazine* could also be good guide words. Words like *many* or *make* would not be good. They are too easy to forget.

Once you have a guide word, you should try to stay with it. You may want to draw a picture of your guide word on an index card and put the letter on the other side. That way you can look at your guide word whenever you have trouble.

If you have trouble thinking of a guide word for any particular letter, we can use the chart below to locate some suggested guide words.

Letter	Page	Letter	Page	Letter	Page	Letter	Page
s	50	c	51	y	53	l	54
f	50	t	51	b	53	d	54
m	50	k	54	z	53	n	51
w	57	g	57	r	57	p	58
j	59	qu	58	h	59	soft c	64
v	58					soft g	64

⑭ TIPS: Read these tips to the student and discuss them with him or her.
REMINDER: Flash cards for the new words are located at the end of the book and can be used at the instructor's discretion.

24 NEW BEGINNINGS IN READING: INSTRUCTOR'S GUIDE

Initial Consonant Activities

Even though all of the initial consonant sounds are presented on these pages at the back of the book, it is suggested that the student work only on the consonants that he finds difficult. The phonics section of the separate *Placement Test*, the pretest at the beginning of *Groundbreaker*, or the **"Tips on How to Improve Your Reading"** can be used to figure out which consonant sounds the student has not mastered.

Picture clues are provided so that the student has something to refer to if he has difficulty with a consonant sound.

There will be times when the student will say that a picture is one thing and the instructor will say that it is another. For example, some students may refer to this picture as a "cap," while others may call it a "hat." The purpose of this exercise is not picture identification, but rather initial consonant identification. If the student calls the picture a "hat" and eliminates it because it does not have the "c" sound as in *cap*, that is a correct response, since the student has correctly discriminated the sound.

Directions at the bottom of the page explain how to use this page. The student should find words in each section that have the same beginning sound as the one in the box and then label the picture with that letter. Pictures of words that do not have the sound in that section should be crossed out.

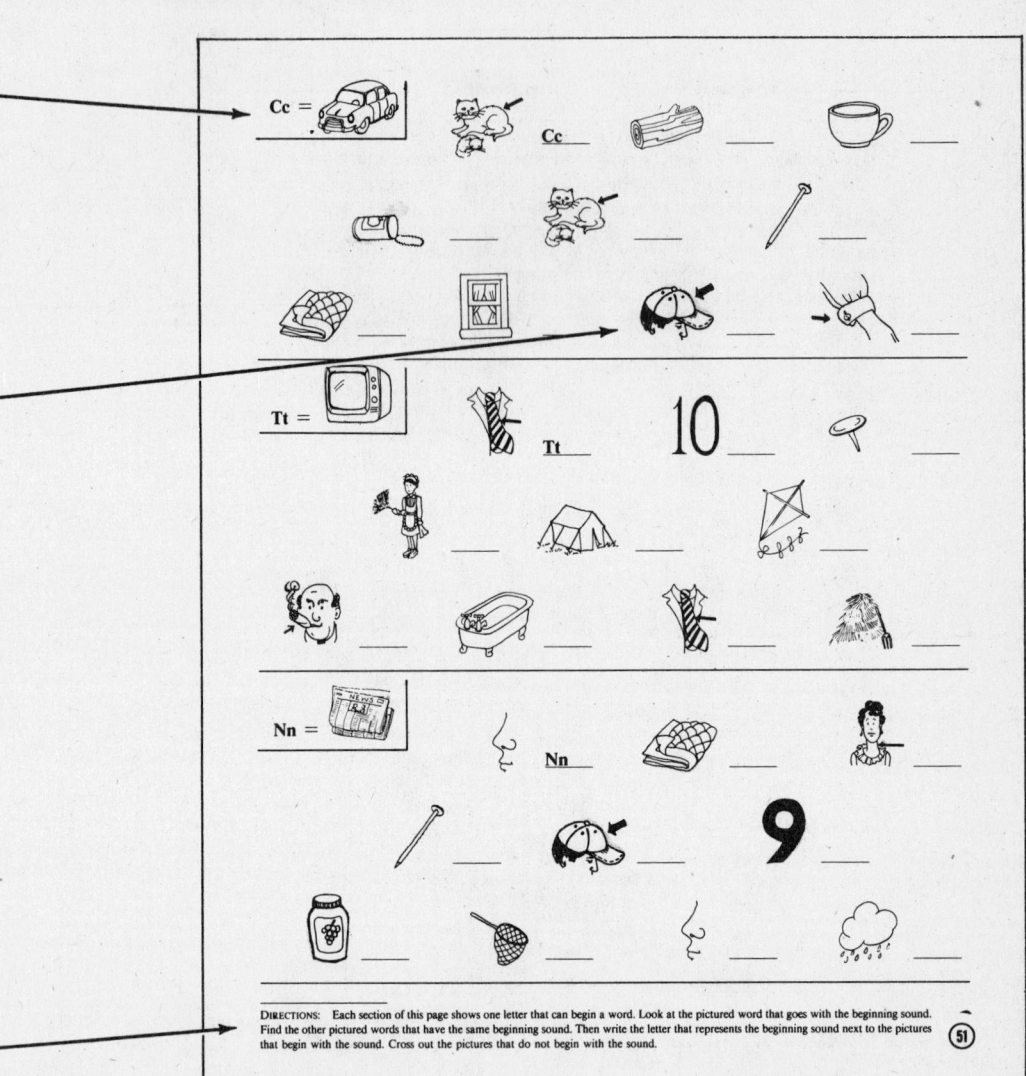

Sample Lessons—Groundbreaker Exercises 25

After the initial consonants have been covered, exercises that compare the different consonant sounds are included so that the student has to differentiate among the different sounds that have been covered.

Picture clues are provided for students to refer to if they need to be reminded of a particular sound.

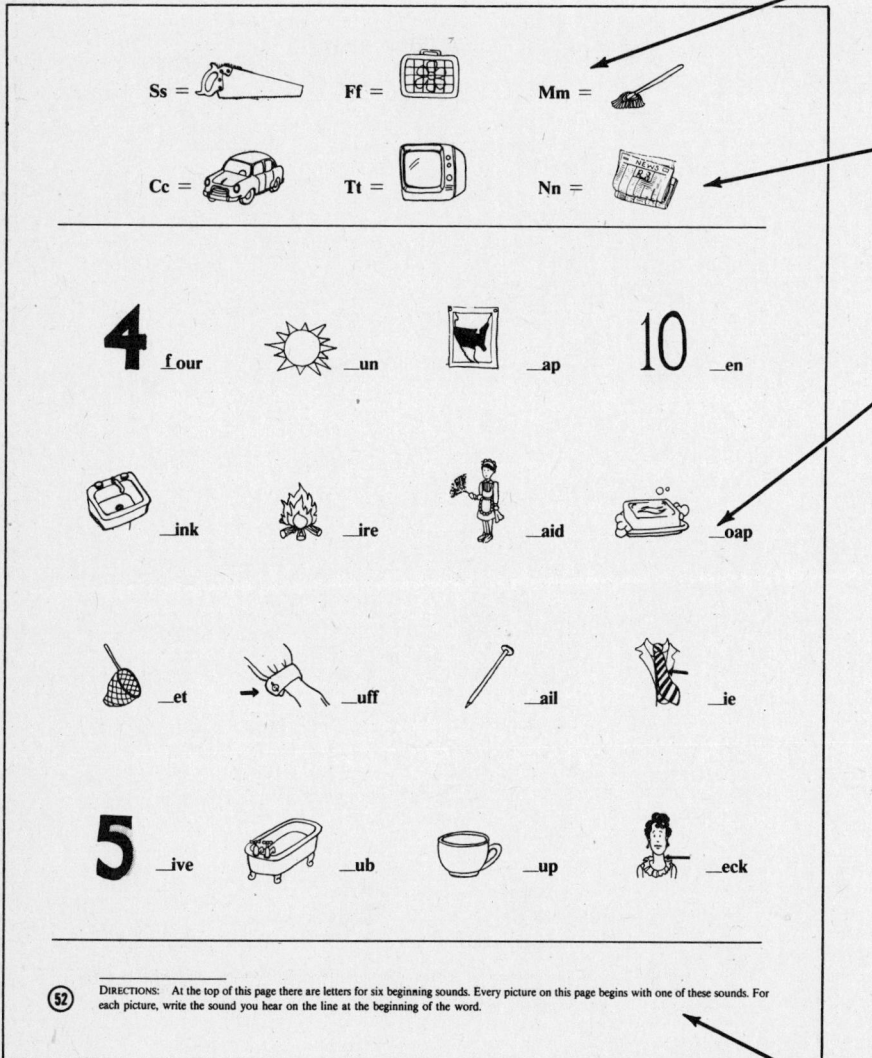

The student is asked to fill in the initial consonant sound for each picture and accompanying word. Although the rest of the word is provided for the student, these words are not to become reading practice. The letters of each word are included so that the student can see how the initial consonant relates to the rest of the word.

When a student gets to this page, he should already know the consonant sounds or should have just learned them. It is suggested that students who need any work on the consonants on this page do the entire page so that they have to differentiate among all of the different initial consonant sounds.

If a student has difficulty with particular consonant sounds in the initial position, he should also complete the work with that consonant in the **Final Consonant Activities.**

The directions at the bottom of the page give general guidelines on how to carry out this activity.

Some students may need additional reinforcement beyond these pages in *New Beginnings*. This reinforcement can be provided with commercially available phonics workbooks or through student/teacher-made materials (see the tip in *Groundbreaker* Lesson 4).

Final Consonant Activities

Even though all of the final consonant sounds are presented on these pages, it is suggested that the student only work on the consonants that he finds difficult. The student should work on the same final consonant sounds that he worked on in the exercises on the initial consonant sounds.

Picture clues are provided for students to refer to if they have difficulty with a final consonant sound.

There will be times when the student will say that a picture is one thing and the instructor will say that it is another. For example, some students may refer to this picture as a "duck," while others may call it a "bird." The purpose of this exercise is not picture identification, but rather the identification of the final consonant sounds. If the student calls the picture "bird" and eliminates it because it does not have the final "k" sound as in *lock*, that is a correct response, since the student has correctly discriminated the sound.

Directions at the bottom of the page explain how to use this page. The student should find words in each section that have the same final consonant sound as the one in the box and then label the picture with that letter. Pictures of words that do not have the sound in that section should be crossed out.

Sample Lessons—Groundbreaker Exercises 27

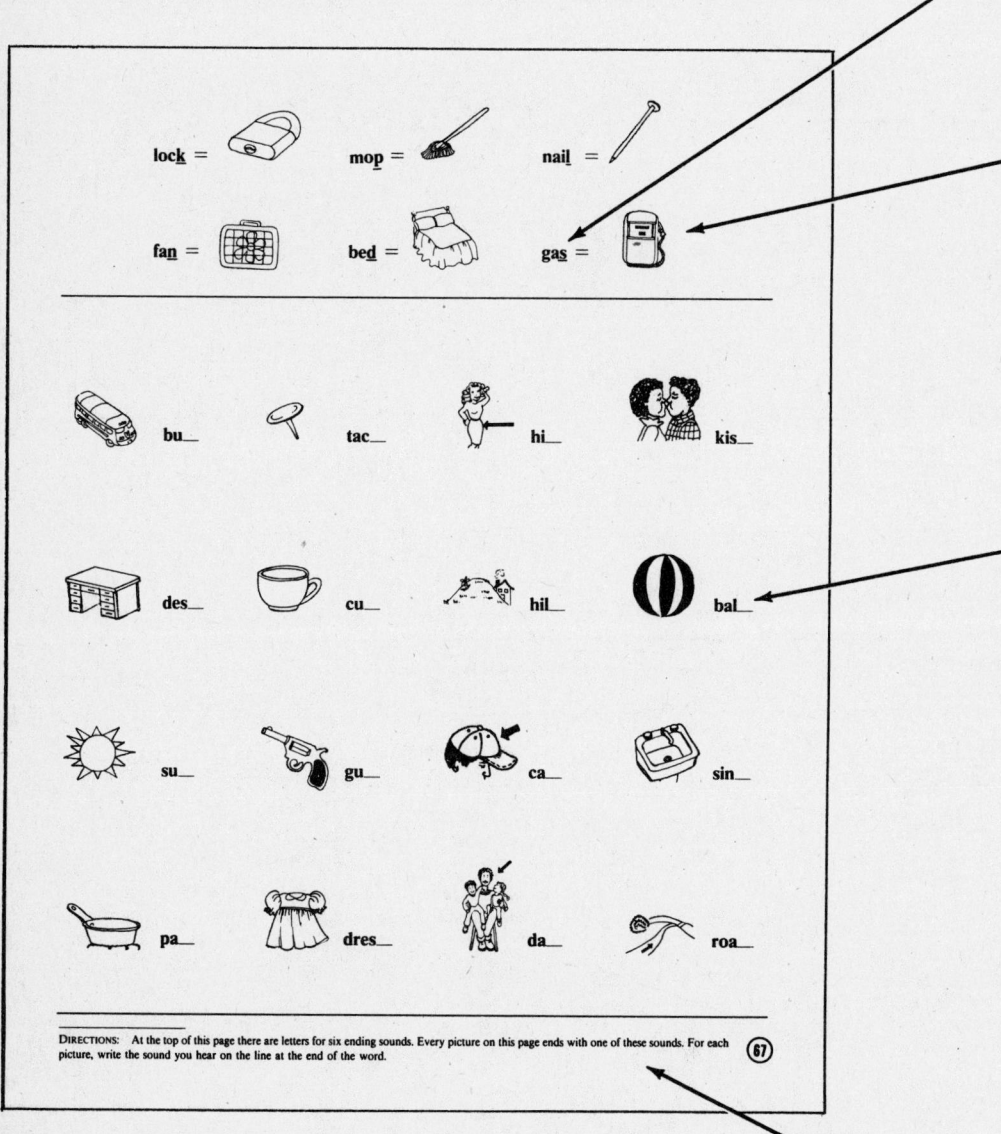

After the final consonants have been covered, exercises that compare the different final consonant sounds are included so that the student has to differentiate among the different sounds that have been covered.

Picture clues are provided for the student to refer to if he needs to be reminded of a particular sound.

The student is asked to fill in the final consonant sound for each picture and accompanying word. Although the beginning portions of the words are provided, these words are not to be used for reading practice. The letters of each word are included so that the student can see how the final consonant relates to the rest of the word.

When a student gets to this page, he should already know the final consonant sounds or should have just learned them. It is suggested that students who need any work on the final consonants on this page do the entire page so that they have to differentiate among all of the different final consonant sounds.

The directions at the bottom of the page give general guidelines on how to carry out this activity.

Some students may need additional reinforcement beyond these pages in *New Beginnings*. This reinforcement can be provided with commercially available phonics workbooks or through student/teacher-made materials (see the tip in *Groundbreaker* Lesson 4).

BOOK 1
Lesson 3

In the odd-numbered books (*Books 1*, *3*, *5*, *7*), adult-oriented themes such as employment, health, housing, consumer economics, and the government are emphasized. After a theme is introduced in a lesson, it serves as a basis for the other readings in the lesson.

Words are introduced by themselves and then in a sentence. The instructor should introduce each new word by reading the word and then reading the first sentence of each accompanying pair of sentences. The student reads the second sentence in each pair. If the student has difficulty reading the new word, the instructor can either say the word for the student or reread the first sentence. It is suggested that new words be reviewed several times in this manner before beginning the next activity.

The new words are used in a sentence so that the student can see how each of them is used. Each of the sentences focuses on the topic presented in the lesson.

Directions at the bottom of the page tell how the instructor should introduce the new words.

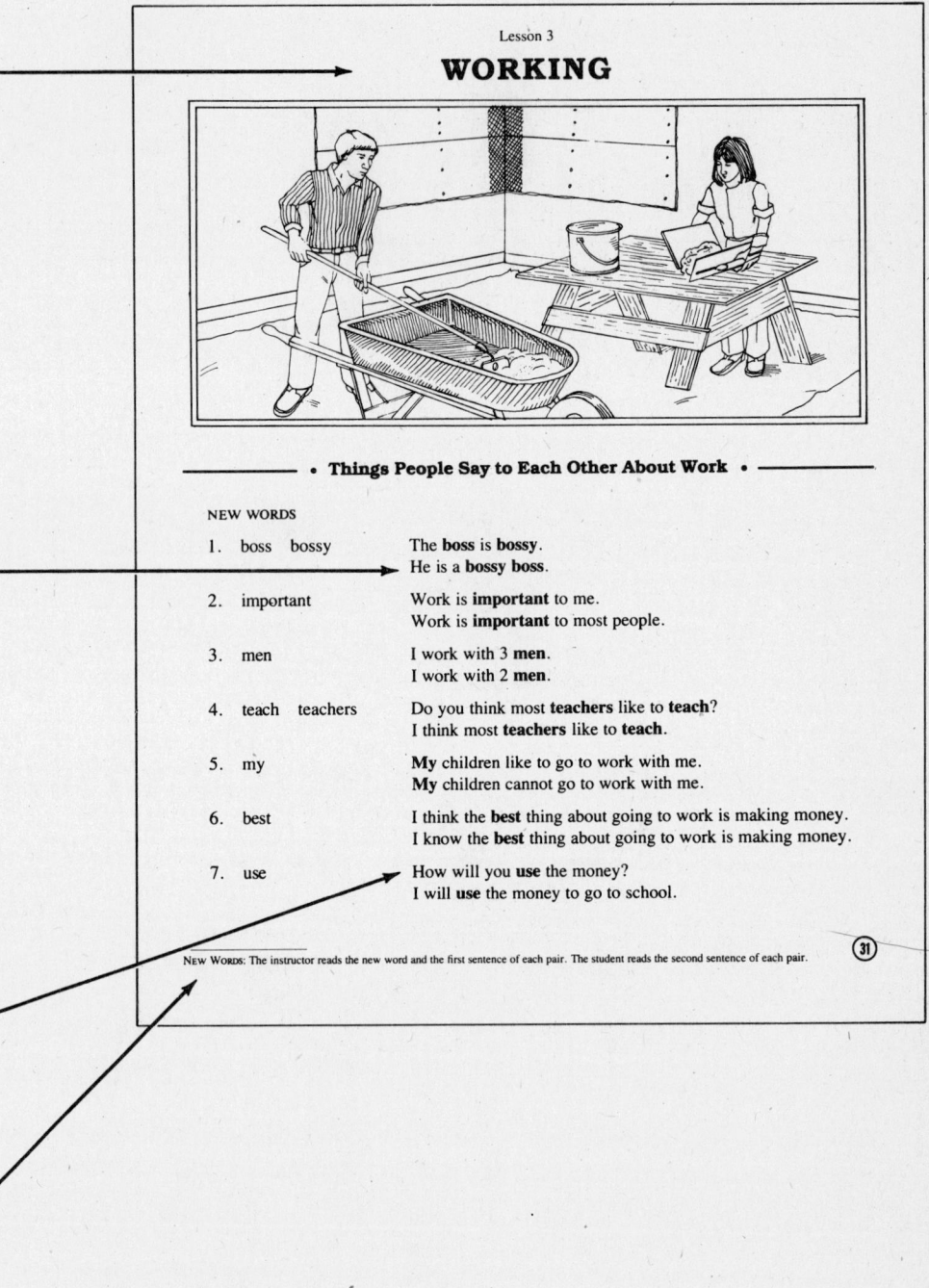

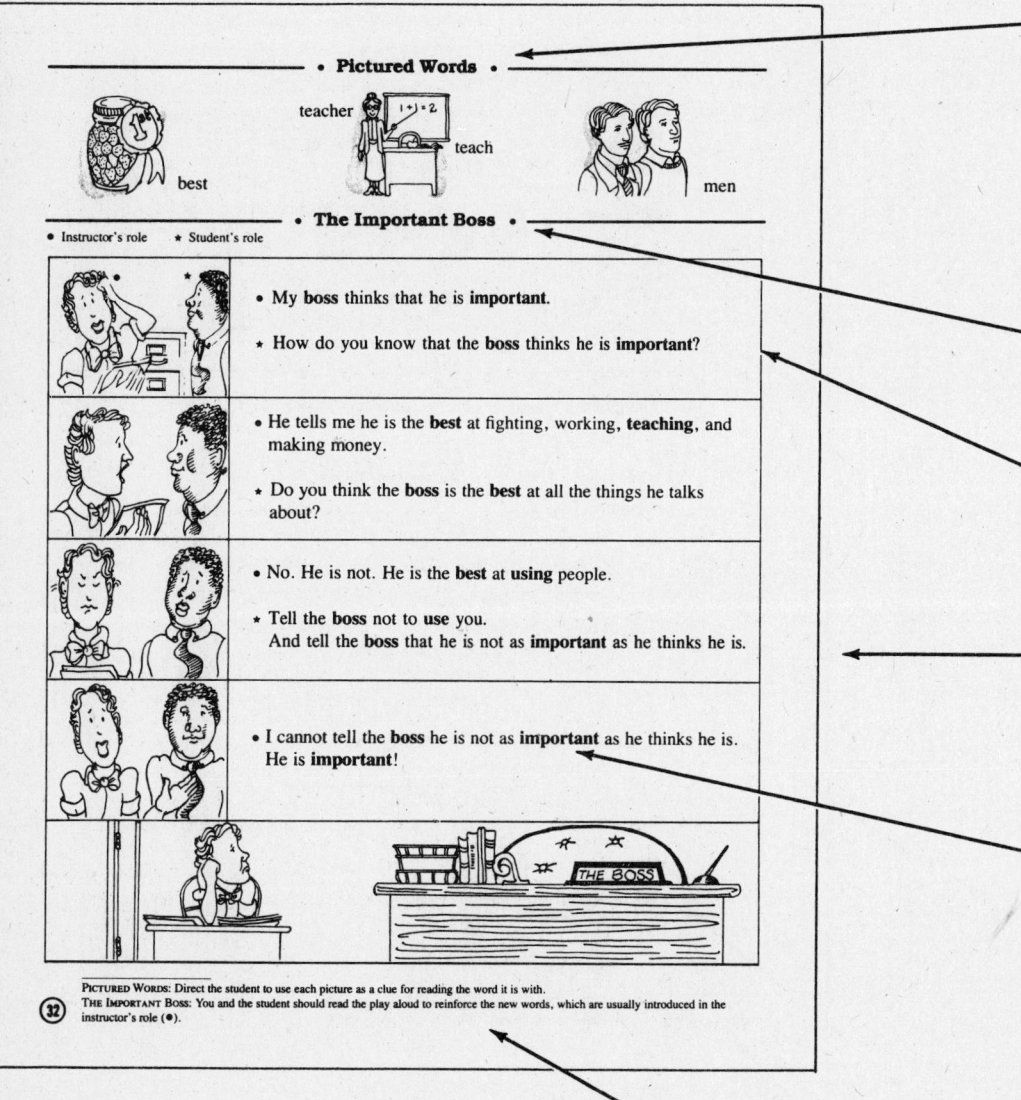

"**Pictured Words**" gives picture cues for some of the new words. Later in this lesson, if the student still has difficulty remembering a new word, she can come back to this page and use the "**Pictured Words**" as cues.

The dots (●) around the titles on this page indicate that this activity requires instructor assistance.

The dot (●) and the star (★) in the first frame indicate the characters that are being portrayed.

In the odd-numbered books, a play is used to reinforce the new words. The instructor's role (●) comes first and reintroduces the new words.

If a student has difficulty with a new word in the play (words in bold print), the instructor can direct the student to the "**Pictured Words**," say the word for the student, or reread her own line to emphasize the new word.

To allow the student to practice with the new words, it is a good idea to read the play two or three times, reversing the roles.

Directions at the bottom of the page show the instructor how to use that page.

"**Tips on How to Improve Your Reading**" are to be read to the student by the instructor. Tips are designed to deal with the adult beginning reader's concerns about the reading process. Tips discuss many issues, from using word families for learning new words to the importance of reading on a consistent basis. It is suggested that the instructor discuss the tips with the student. The instructor and the student can evaluate the tips in terms of their usefulness and discuss strategies for their implementation.

"**Skill Building**" is instructor-assisted, as indicated by the dots. Skill Building gives the student an opportunity to review old skills and develop new ones. The answers to "**Skill Building**" can be found in the answer key near the back of each book.

The student uses the meaning of a short paragraph to determine which words should be inserted in the blanks. The ability to use the meaning of a sentence is an important skill for all readers. If the student has difficulty with this exercise, the instructor may write similar exercises, but with only one word missing.

The "**Good Reader**" statements are to be read to the student. They explain why the skills the student is learning are important in the reading process.

Compound words are built from smaller words that the student already has in her reading vocabulary. The student should read each compound word and then circle the smaller words that make it.

Using the student's reading vocabulary, words and word parts are combined to form new words.

Directions explain how this page is to be used.

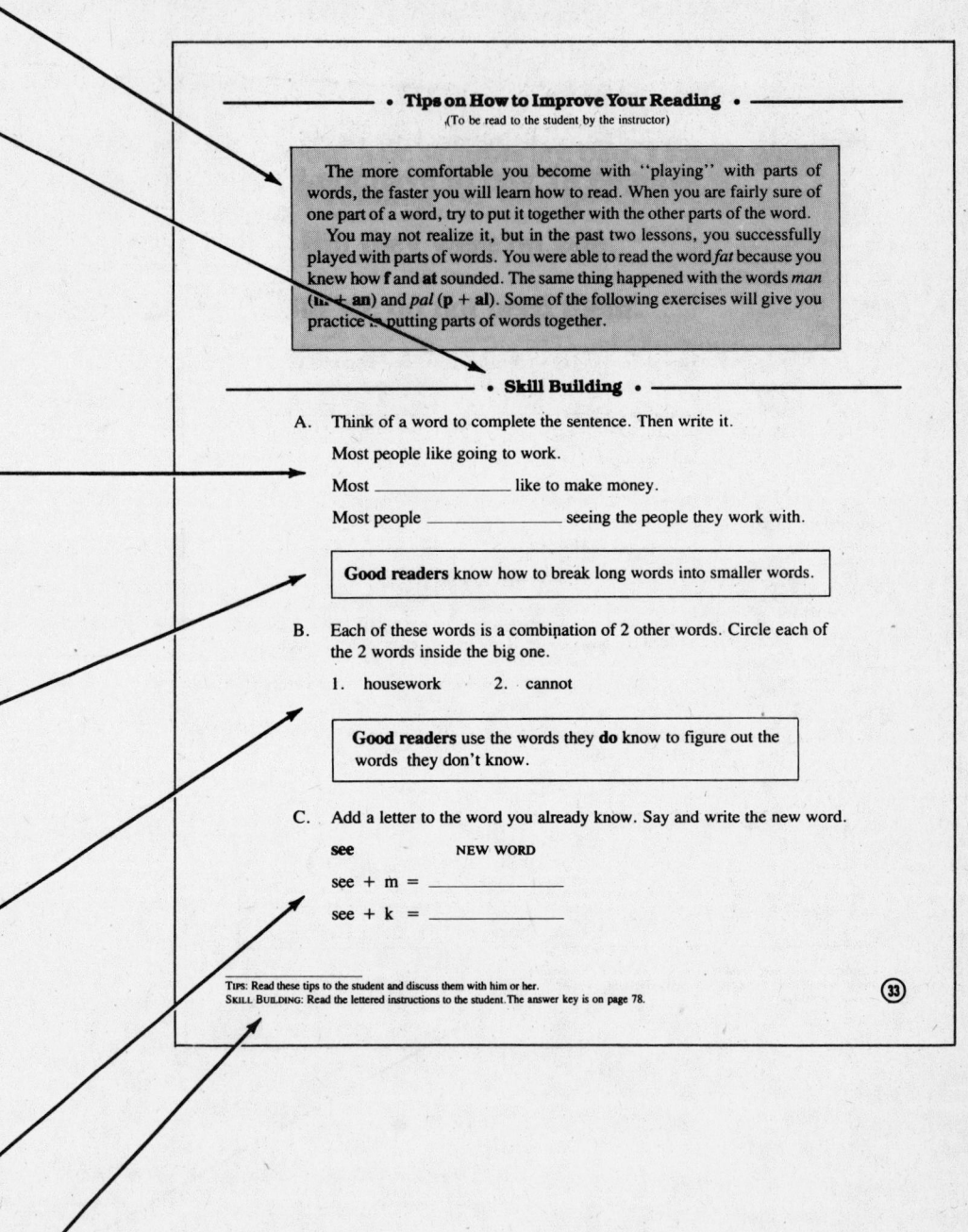

The continuation of the "Skill Building" activities.

D. Put each word in the shape that fits it.

use
my

E. Read each sentence and write the word that completes it.

men　important　boss　teach　my　use　best

1. The b _ _ _ has money.
2. I am going to see m _ friends.
3. I will u _ _ her money.
4. He is going to be my b _ _ _ man.
5. The m _ _ have to go to work.
6. Can you t _ _ _ _ me how to play music?
7. He is i _ _ _ _ _ _ _ _ to me.

F. To learn **ing** and **ly** endings, write the correct word.

1. He is _____ my house.
   used　using
2. She is _____ .
   jealous　jealously
3. Her friends are _____ music.
   teach　teaching
4. He talks _____ .
   jealous　jealously

G. Read the sentences. Then write the words that are in **bold print**.

I am married. I **have** children.
I have friends. I work.
I go to school. I have **all** the **things** I want.

h_____　a_____　th_____

H. Circle the word that is repeated each time you see it.

1. Do you have some use for the mat?　　2. He is my boss.
   I will use a van.　　　　　　　　　　　　Do not boss me.

㉞ ADDITIONAL REINFORCEMENT: When the student is comfortable with the new words in this lesson, the flash cards at the end of the book can be used for reinforcement.

Students are asked to look at the shape of a word and then place it in the correct set of boxes. This can serve as a memory aid for many beginning readers.

The student is asked to use the meaning of each sentence to determine which word goes in the blank. This exercise uses all of the new words from this lesson so that the student has a chance to practice with these new vocabulary words.

Learning how to use the meaning of a sentence to determine the meaning of an unfamiliar word is very useful for beginning readers. Using sentence meaning is one of the basic methods that a reader applies to unfamiliar words in order to figure them out.

The **-ing** and **-ly** endings are taught by asking the student to select the correct word for each sentence. This gives the student another tool for working with unknown words.

Words from previous lessons are reviewed. After reading the short paragraph, the student writes the words that are in bold print.

Words with multiple meanings are shown so that the student will realize that she will need to use the meaning of the sentence to know how the word is used. The student circles the word that appears more than once in each set of sentences. The instructor may ask the student to note how the circled word is used differently in each sentence.

Directions at the bottom of the page remind the instructor that flash cards are available at the back of the book for the new words from this lesson.

The **Quiz** contains open-ended questions related to the topic of the lesson. These questions ask the student to give her opinion on a topic and then see how other people feel about the same issue. As you get to know your student, these questions can serve as the basis for some interesting discussions.

After the student has answered the quiz questions, the student should compare her responses with other people's opinions. The instructor should emphasize that the student's opinions on the topic are important, even though the student may not agree with what other people think.

The student writes whatever she wants to about the topic of the lesson. In the first few books in *New Beginnings*, some students will need to dictate their sentences to the instructor. The instructor should write the sentences on a separate piece of paper and then let the student copy them into the book. In the later books, students should be able to write their own sentences, with some assistance on spelling.

Students are asked to circle the words that they think of when they think about a specific topic. There is no right or wrong answer. If a student circles a word that you do not associate with the topic, use this as a basis for discussion.

The directions are included at the bottom of the page. For this particular page, the directions note that the quiz may be assigned as independent work.

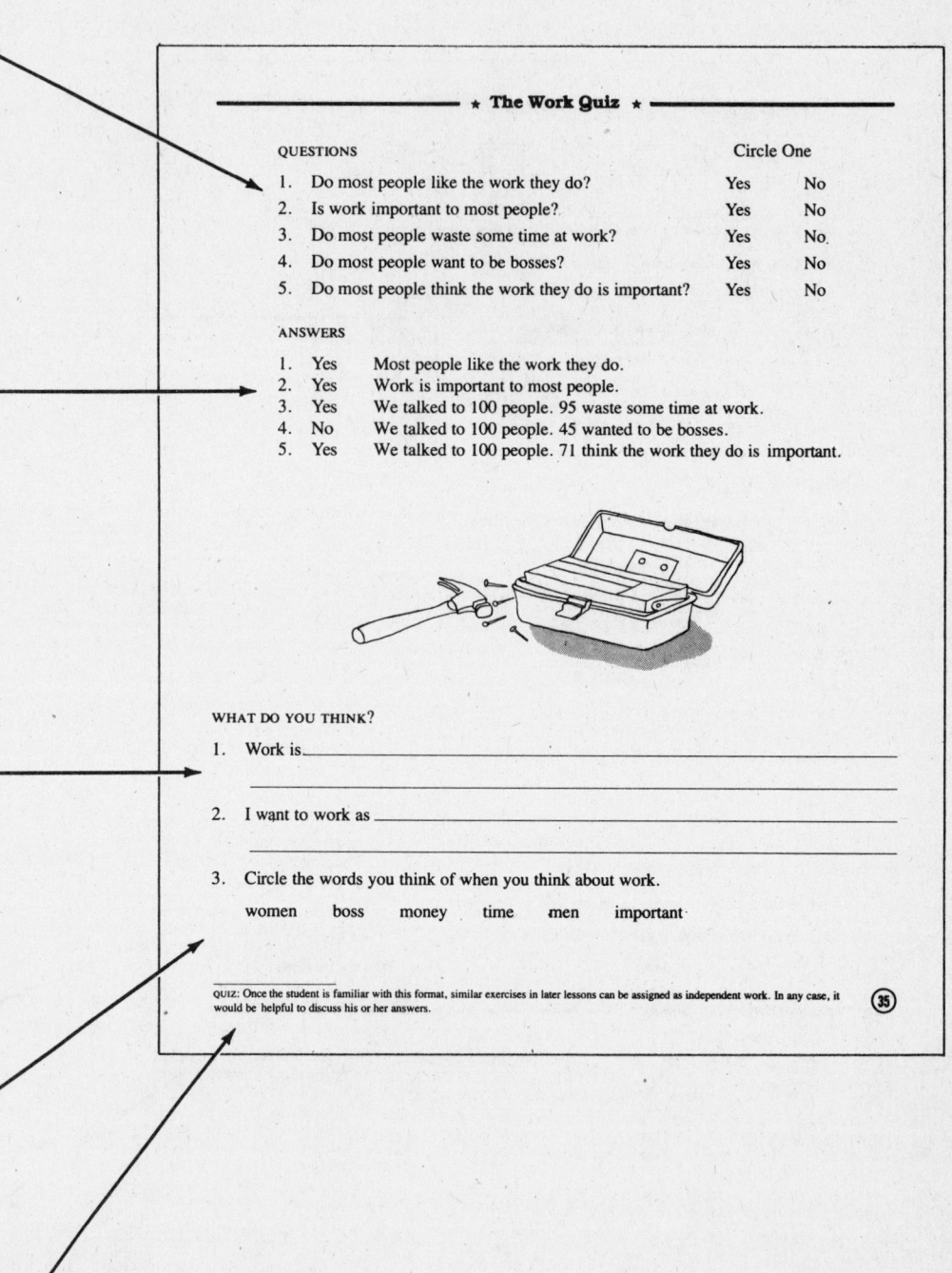

★ Reading to Know Others ★

These 4 students are writing about their work.

Will writes: I am a boss at work. I do not like some things about being a boss. Sometimes I have to tell the men to work. Sometimes the men fight. The best thing about being a boss is the money.

Ann writes: I like the work I do. I am a music teacher. I love music and I like being with people.

Sam writes: The people I work with are like a family. We fight. We yell. We play.

Mike writes: I like to talk with the men at work about 3 things . . . girls, girls, and girls.

WHAT DO YOU THINK?

Sometimes you can tell something about people from the things they write. Have you learned anything about Will, Ann, Sam, and Mike? Read the questions and circle your answers.

1. Does Will like being a boss?   Yes   No   Maybe
2. Is Ann an OK teacher?   Yes   No   Maybe
3. Does Sam like work?   Yes   No   Maybe
4. Does Mike like the men he works with?   Yes   No   Maybe

READING TO KNOW OTHERS: The student should read what each person says and then answer the questions. When the student is comfortable with the format, similar exercises in other lessons can be assigned as independent work. When discussing the answers to "What do you think?" with the student, accept any response that seems reasonable.

REMINDER: Flash cards for the new words are located at the end of the book and can be used at the instructor's discretion.

The stars near the "**Reading to Know Others**" title indicate that the instructor may have the student do this exercise on her own, if the instructor feels that the student can handle this material.

In the odd-numbered books, four students talk about their reactions to topics in that lesson. Each of these characters is presented at least twenty times throughout the series so that the student becomes familiar with the personality of each of the characters.

In "**What Do You Think?**" the student reads four questions that ask the students to draw conclusions about the four characters. The student should be encouraged to re-read the statements and consider the reason behind her answer. The instructor should accept any response that seems reasonable.

The directions at the bottom of the page give the instructor guidelines on how to use this exercise.

Dots around the title indicate that "**Time to Write**" is an instructor-assisted activity.

"**Time To Write**" is a structured language-experience activity. In "**Time To Write**," the student reads several examples of writings on a topic. In this lesson, workers have written suggestions to a boss. The student is then asked to write about the topic. The instructor should assist the student with spelling any words that she needs help with.

In the earlier books, if the student has difficulty generating ideas, the student may copy one of the models word for word. If the student has difficulty writing, he or she may dictate his or her thoughts to the instructor. The instructor should write the student's thoughts on a separate piece of paper and then let the student copy it into the book. Students who dictate their writings should be encouraged to do their own writing as they move through later books in *New Beginnings*.

The directions at the bottom of the page give the instructor suggestions on how to present this activity to the student.

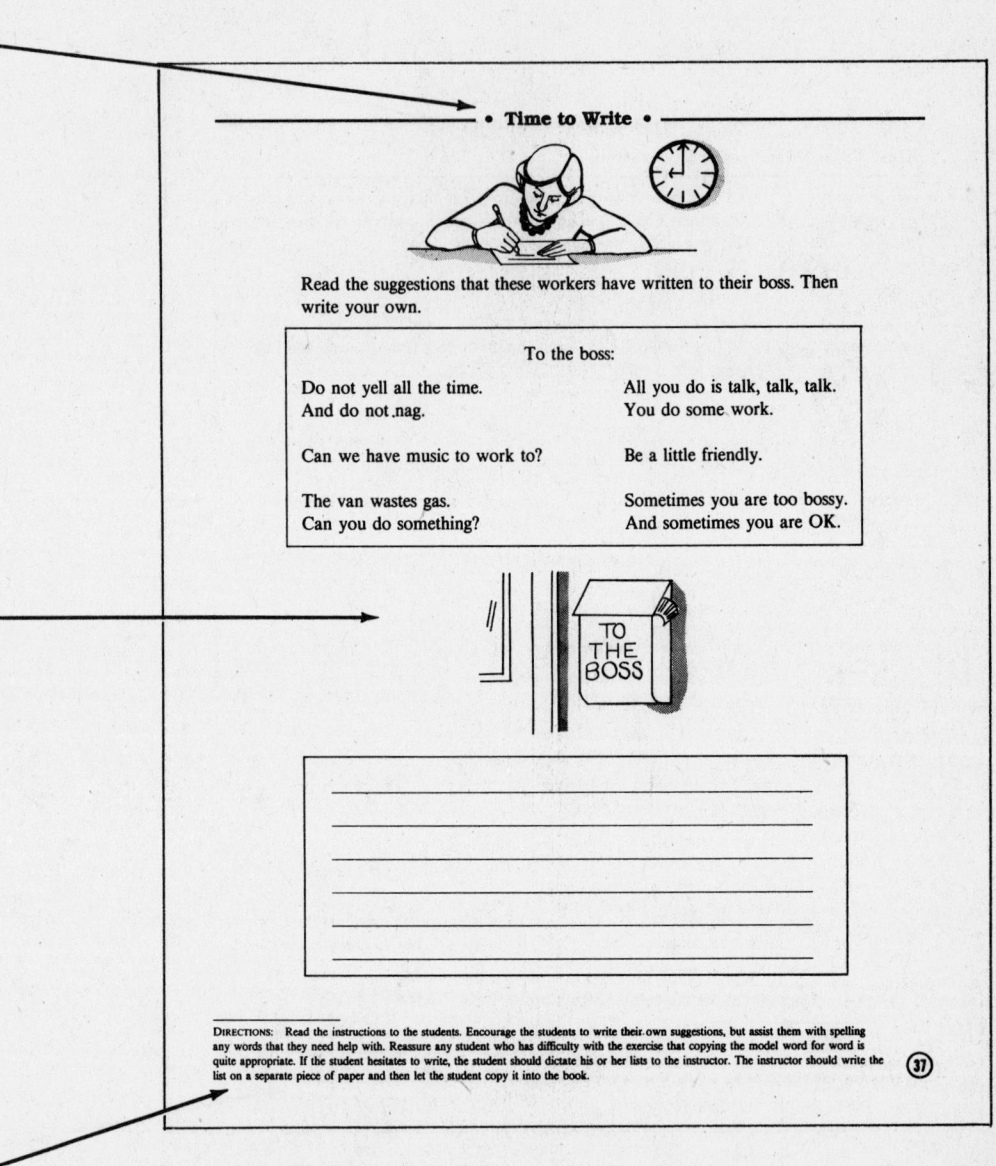

Sample Lessons—Book 1   35

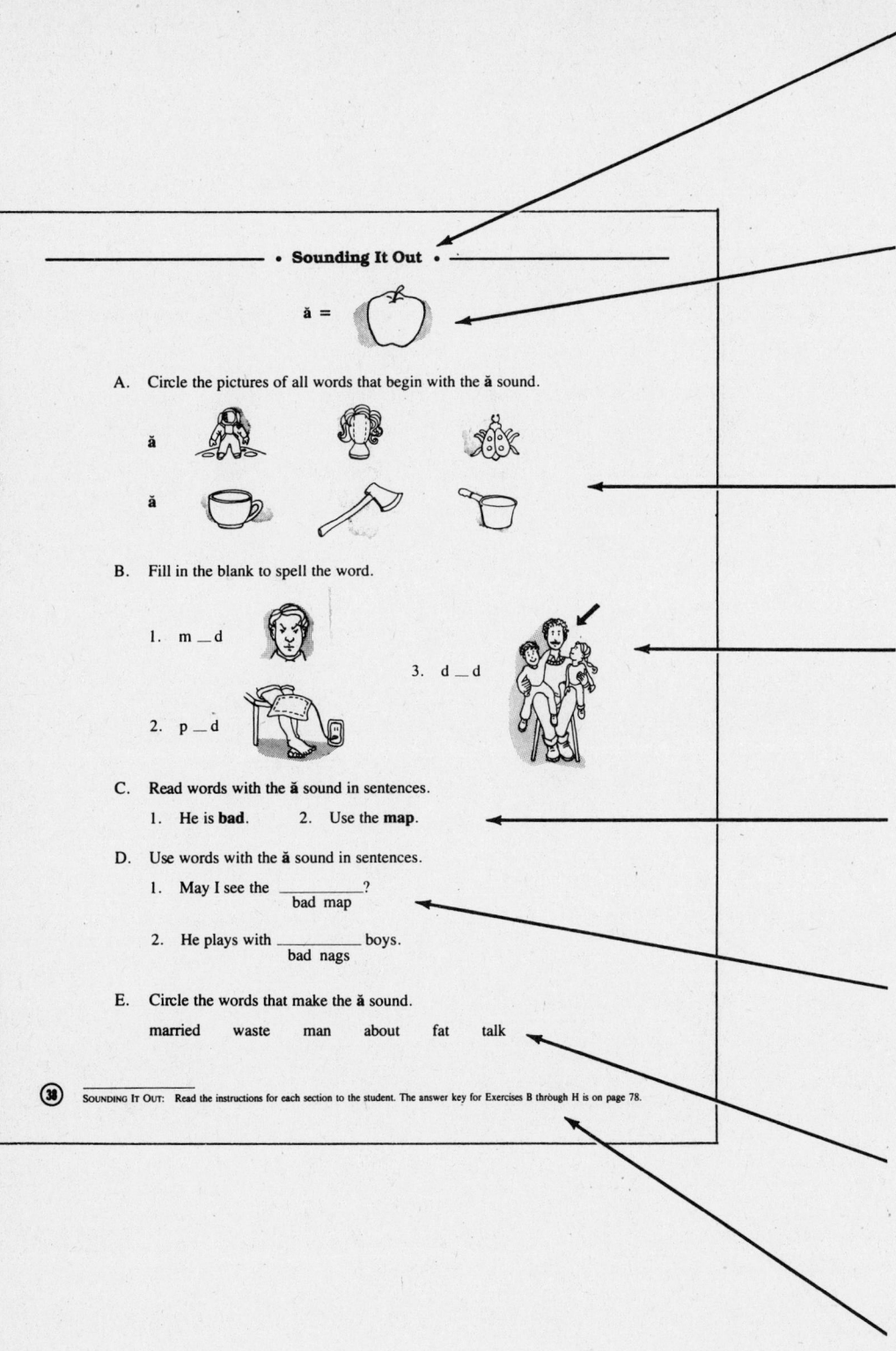

Dots around the title indicate that "**Sounding It Out**" is an instructor-assisted activity.

A picture cue is provided to help the student remember the sound being taught. This lesson covers the short **a** sound. The instructor may want to review the word with the student so that the student will remember the sound and the cue.

The student is asked to circle the pictures of words beginning with the sound that is covered in this lesson.

The student looks at each of the pictures and puts the correct letter in the blank to complete the new word.

The student reads two sentences that have new words based on the sound covered in this lesson.

The student selects the correct word to complete the sentence. This exercise reinforces words with the sound that is covered in this lesson.

The student is asked to identify and circle the words that contain the sound taught in the lesson.

Directions at the bottom of the page give the instructor general guidelines on how these activities should be carried out.

In each **"Sounding It Out"** exercise, word families (rhyming words) are presented that use the sound being covered in the lesson. The word families have three purposes: (1) they reinforce the sounds that are presented in the lesson, (2) they give the student an effective tool for identifying unknown words, and (3) they increase the student's reading vocabulary in a painless, efficient manner.

The word families are reinforced by having the student think of a sentence for the words in each word family. To make the activity more challenging, the instructor may ask the student to incorporate more than one word family word in a sentence.

The words in each word family are reinforced when the student fills in the blank with the correct word.

This exercise may be handled in two different ways. For students who are highly motivated to learn how to spell, this exercise may be conducted as a spelling test. For students who are not inclined toward spelling, the instructor can read a word from the word family lists; then the student can either find and copy the word from the word list or attempt to spell the word without referring to the list.

Since the directions to the student are very clear, the directions remind the instructor that the spelling words should be taken from the word families at the top of the page.

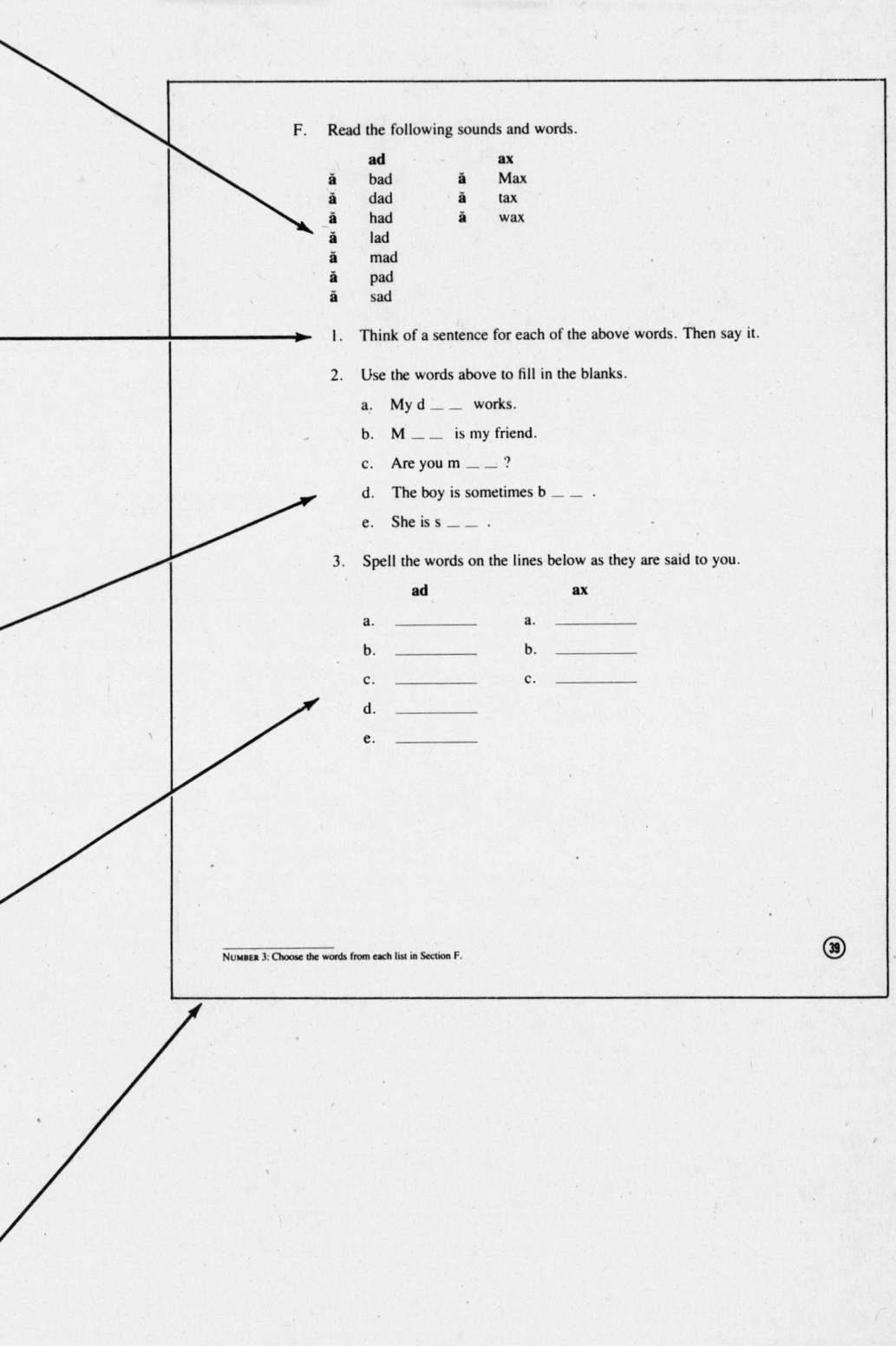

Sample Lessons—Book 1   37

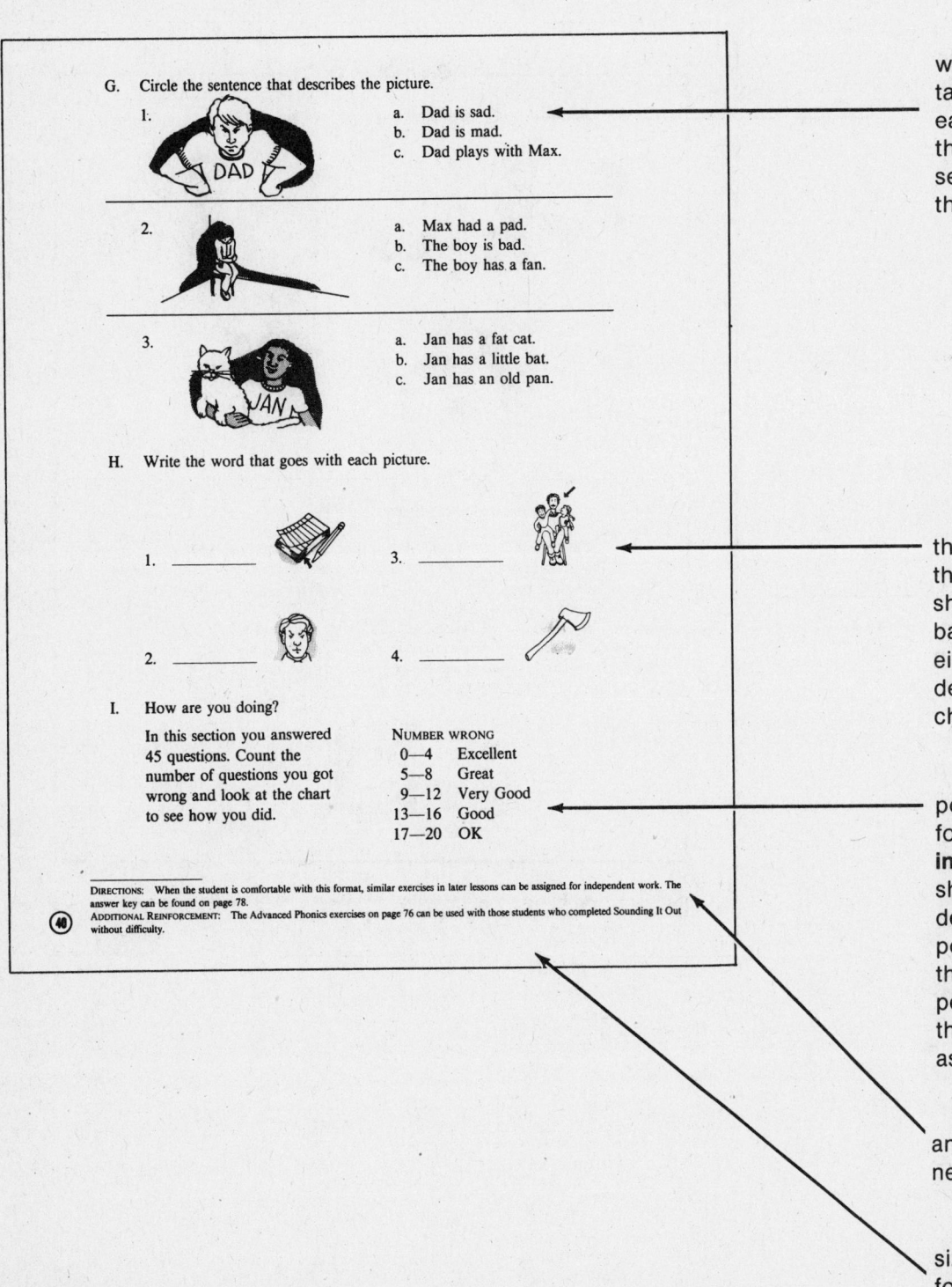

To reinforce the words in the word families that were just taught, the student looks at each picture and reads the three sentences, selecting the sentence that best describes the picture.

The student writes the word that describes each picture. If the student has difficulty, she should be encouraged to look back to the earlier exercises, either to find the word that describes the picture or to check the spelling of the word.

The student is given the opportunity to evaluate her performance at the end of "**Sounding It Out**." The instructor should remember that students need a large amount of positive reinforcement, even if their performance is less than perfect. Emphasize the ways that the student is improving as a reader.

The directions indicate that an answer key can be found near the back of the book.

Additional exercises emphasizing the word families can be found in the **Advanced Phonics Exercises** near the back of the book. These are intended for students who are oriented toward a phonics approach.

While this lesson gives the general format of the "**Sounding It Out**" exercises, the instructor should be aware that the **Phonics Exercises** in later books do include several variations.

It is strongly suggested that the **"On Your Own"** activities be assigned for independent work. The **"On Your Own"** exercises usually consist of the last three to five pages of each lesson. While students should be encouraged to do the activities on their own, the instructor may want to follow up these activities by discussing the stories with the student.

The **"On Your Own"** activities vary from book to book, but the exercises within each book follow a similar format from lesson to lesson.

The student is directed to look at five pictures and circle the things that she likes. This particular exercise is about work. Each of these exercises could be used as the basis for interesting discussions. For instance, in this exercise about work, the following questions could be discussed: What things do you like about work? What things do you dislike? Do all jobs have advantages and disadvantages? What is the best job you ever had?

Each lesson contains several short readings. This exercise is about a reading teacher and how she perceives herself, her job, and her students. Each of these readings can serve as the basis for an interesting discussion. For this lesson, the following questions can be discussed: What do you think of this person? Have you ever known anyone like her? Do you respect her?

The directions in the **"On Your Own"** exercises suggest that these exercises be assigned as independent work as soon as the student is able to do them by herself.

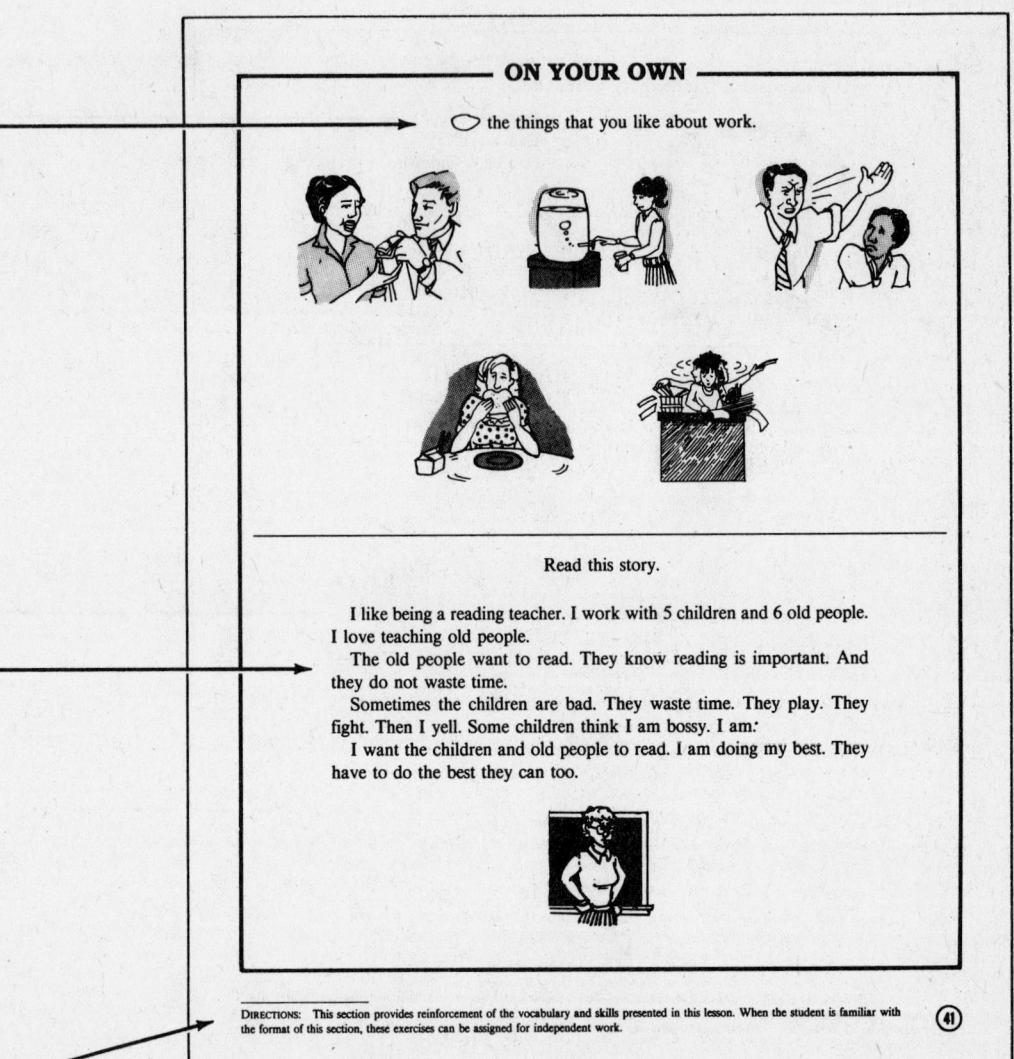

ON YOUR OWN

★ Married to Work ★

The man I married is married to work. I am married to Hal. He goes to work at 6 a.m. He works to 9 p.m.

I talked to Hal about all the time he worked. He had no time for me. He had no time for the children. I wanted Hal to play with the children.

I talked to Hal about how important the family is. Hal talked to me about how important work is.

I yelled, and Hal worked. I nagged, and Hal worked.

Then I used my mind. The children and I see Hal all the time. We go to see Hal at work.

★ Talking to the Boss ★

Max and Jan are friends. They are talking about the work they do.

Max: I have to talk to my boss about something.
Jan: We are friends. Tell me.

Max: I am mad at the boss.
Jan: Tell me the things that she does to make you mad.

Max: Sometimes she uses me.
Jan: How does she use you?

Max: She tells me that I do the best work.
Jan: And you are mad at her?

Max: She tells me that she likes my work.
Then she wants me to do her work, too.
Jan: You do not have to talk to the boss.
You have to talk to the boss's boss.

(42) TWO READING EXERCISES: These exercises provide reinforcement and can be assigned as independent work.

It is suggested that "**On Your Own**" activities be assigned for independent work as soon as the student is able to do the work on her own.

Each "**On Your Own**" contains several readings that reinforce the vocabulary that has been presented up to this point in *New Beginnings*. This particular story shows how a woman who is married to a workaholic deals with his behavior. The instructor may want to follow up the reading of these stories with several discussion questions. Possible discussion questions for this story are: Do you know anyone who spends all of his or her time working? What happens when someone does not make time for friends or family? Did the woman in the story deal with the problem correctly?

After the student has had a chance to read the play to herself and is familiar with it, the play can be read in parts with the instructor or another student, with each one taking a part.

Directions at the bottom of the page suggest that the readings in "**On Your Own**" be assigned as independent work.

"**On Your Own**" activities should be assigned as independent work as soon as the student is capable of doing the exercises on her own.

"**Playing with Words**" contains several fun activities, which are designed to reinforce the vocabulary words from this and previous lessons.

The word find reinforces the new words from each lesson by presenting them in a sentence and then in the word find. This is usually one of the most popular activities in each lesson, as it is invariably a successful experience for the student.

The student is directed to put the scrambled words into a sequence that forms a sentence. If a student experiences difficulty, it is suggested that the instructor place all but two or three of the words into the proper sequence. As the student works through *New Beginnings*, the instructor should give less and less assistance on this type of exercise, until the student can do it without any assistance.

The crossword puzzle uses the "**Pictured Words**" from the second page of each lesson as clues. Several of the new words from each lesson are reinforced. The initial letter for each word is provided so that the student will not have difficulty with the placement of each word.

The directions indicate that the answer key for the "**Playing with Words**" activities is located near the back of the book.

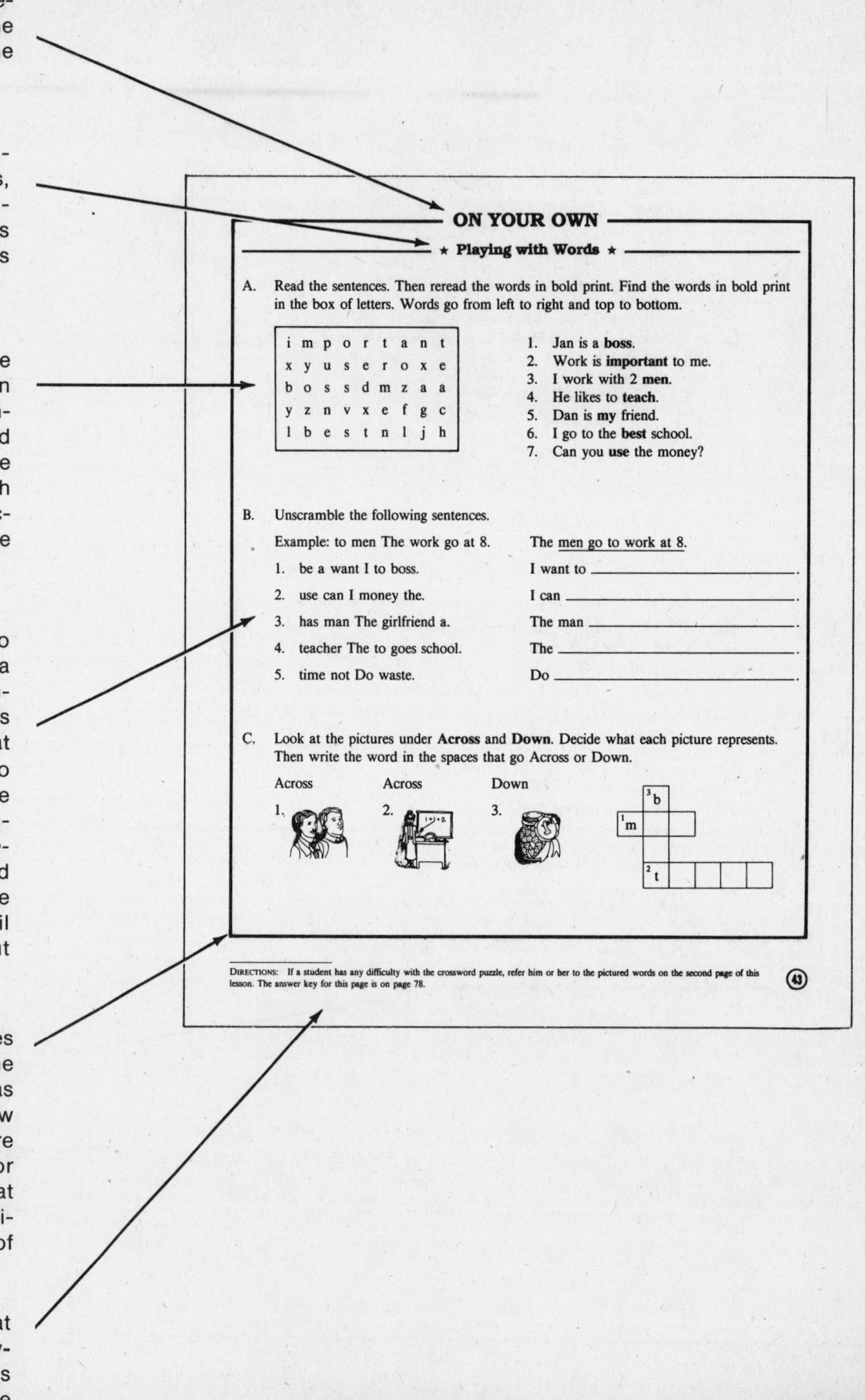

ON YOUR OWN
★ Time to Buy ★

A. Who will buy it?

Look at the picture. Put a ✔ next to the people who are most likely to buy the things pictured.

___ 1. people that have children   ___ 4. a girl that loves music
___ 2. a music teacher   ___ 5. a man that loves school
___ 3. a boy that fights   ___ 6. a boy that loves to talk

B. What does she need?

Jan is a boss at work. Sometimes she works at her house. ◯ the things that she has to have.

1.   2.   3.   4.

C. Should you buy it?

Read the things below and see if you should buy the TV.

    A. J. tells you 3 things.

    1. Schools use TVs.
    2. The TV can teach **you** things.
    3. You can have the TV for $250.

    You know 1 thing.

    1. You have $159 for a TV.

    Can you buy the TV? _____
                               yes or no

DIRECTIONS: Read the instructions for Exercises A and C to the student. All exercises can be assigned for independent work when the student is familiar with the format. The word "buy" has been used in Exercise C even though it has not been formally presented. The answer key is on page 78.

"**On Your Own**" activities can be assigned as independent work.

"**Time to Buy**," a feature of the "**On Your Own**" exercises in *Book 1*, presents three exercises related to consumer economics.

The student is asked to draw a conclusion about which people are most likely to buy the object shown in the picture. Even though "**Time to Buy**" is found only in the lessons in *Book 1*, the exercises are identical in format.

The student is given some information about a person's life and then is asked to circle the pictures of the items that the person needs.

In "Should You Buy It?" the student confronts a salesman named AJ, who gives the student three reasons to buy the TV set. In Lessons 1-4, the student should be encouraged to be sales-resistant, as the TV costs more than the student is told that he can afford.

The directions at the bottom of the page give general guidelines for these activities.

The "**On Your Own**" activities should be assigned as independent work. The instructor may want to discuss the activity with the student after the student has read the story.

This "**On Your Own**" activity is included in all of the lessons in Book 1. Besides this story, there are readings entitled "Reading, the Family, and Me", "Reading, Money, and Me"; "Reading, Friends, and Me"; and "Reading, Free Time, and Me."

In the first two pictures in the story, an adult has a reading problem that interferes with his daily activities.

In the picture in the middle of the page, the adult goes back to school to learn to read.

In the last two pictures, the adult is able to read and is able to do activities that he used to have difficulty with.

This activity can be used as the basis for some interesting discussions. After looking at the pictures and reading the captions, the student may feel comfortable sharing with the instructor how reading prevented her from achieving certain goals in the past and how she believes that education will affect her future.

Directions at the bottom of this page give general guidance on this activity.

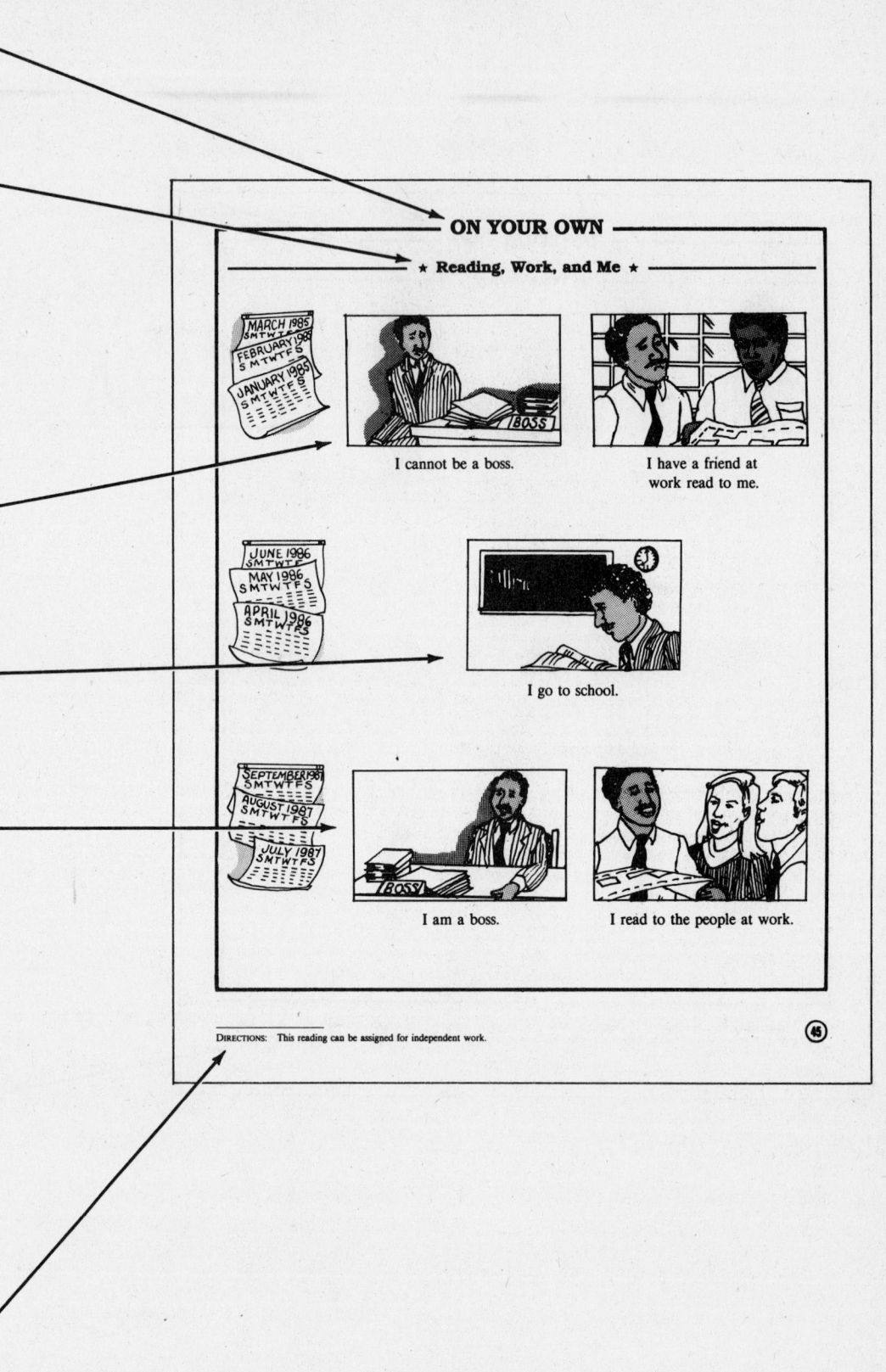

BOOK 2
Lesson 2

Each of the even-numbered books (*Books 2, 4, 6,* and *8*), has the following pattern:
  Lesson 1—facts related to literacy are presented
  Lesson 2—the story of a famous person who did not learn to read until he or she was older
  Lesson 3—reviews of books that focus on the reading process
  Lesson 4—the story of a famous person who had a learning disability
  Lesson 5—students talk about why they never learned to read (*Book 2*), why they came back to school (*Book 4*), how they feel about learning to read (*Book 6*), and their future plans (*Book 8*)

Lesson 2

WOODROW WILSON

• Things to Think About When You Read Lesson 2 •

NEW WORDS

1. president — How many **presidents** have we had?
   What does the **president** do?
2. was were — How old **was** the 28th president when he learned to read?
   How old **were** you when you learned to read?
3. world — What did the people of the **world** think of Woodrow Wilson?
   What do you think of Woodrow Wilson?
4. made — Do you think Woodrow Wilson **made** many friends for the U.S.A?
   How do you think he **made** friends for the U.S.A.?
5. war — What **war** did the U.S.A. fight in 1917?
   What **war** did the U.S.A. fight in the 1960s and 1970s?
6. went — When the U.S.A. **went** to war in 1917, did most of the people want war?
   When the U.S.A. **went** to war in the 1960s, did most of the people want war?
7. from — What did Woodrow Wilson learn **from** his father?
   What do you want to learn **from** reading about Woodrow Wilson?

(16) NEW WORDS: The instructor reads the new word and the first sentence of each pair. The student reads the second sentence of each pair.

Words are introduced by themselves and then in a sentence. The instructor should introduce each new word by reading the new word and then reading the first sentence of each accompanying pair of sentences. The student reads the second sentence in each pair. If the student has difficulty reading the new word, the instructor can either say the word for the student or reread the first sentence.

The new words are used in a sentence so that the student can see how each of them is used. Each of the sentences focuses on the topic presented in the lesson.

Directions at the bottom of the page tell how the instructor should introduce the new words.

43

The dot next to the title for this page indicates that this is an instructor-assisted activity.

If the student seems to be comfortable with the new words, the student may read the selection silently to himself, and then read it orally. The instructor should assist the student with any difficult words.

If the student is not comfortable with the new words, the instructor may read the passage to the student while the student follows in his book. The instructor may also read the selection with the student. After they read the passage together, the student should read it independently.

The directions at the bottom of the page indicate that this is an instructor-assisted activity.

• Important People: Woodrow Wilson •

From 1788 to 1985, the people of the U.S.A. had 40 presidents. Woodrow Wilson was the 28th president of the U.S.A. He learned to read when he was 11.

When he was a boy, Woodrow Wilson did not like school. His dad was his best friend. He was his best teacher, too. Woodrow Wilson learned many things from his dad. He learned to work for what was important.

At 29, Woodrow was a teacher. At 46, he was made president of Princeton University. Then at 56, he was made president of the U.S.A.

As president, Wilson worked for the working man. He wanted all the people of the world to be free. He did many things to make all people free.

From 1912 to 1916 Wilson did not want the U.S.A. to go to war. But in 1917, most of the people wanted to go to war. Wilson wanted the U.S.A. to go to war, too. And the U.S.A. went to war.

Wilson was a good president in the war. But he did not want another war. He did not want the children to see another war.

The people of the world loved Wilson. But the people of the U.S.A. did not. They did not want to think about war. They did not want to think about other people. They were mad at Wilson. They did not make Woodrow Wilson president in 1920.

Woodrow Wilson was president from 1912 to 1920. Woodrow Wilson was 1 of the best presidents the U.S.A. has had.

READING SELECTION: The student reads the passage with instructor assistance, if necessary.

⑰

Sample Lessons—Book 2 45

The stars next to the title indicate that this exercise may be assigned as independent work.

The student is asked to write another title for the story. This helps the student to understand the main idea of the story. For this particular page, the student could generate titles such as "A Good President" or "An Important President." The instructor may need to assist the student with spelling any difficult words.

Statements are made about the story, and the student is asked to circle "Yes" if the statement is true and "No" if the statement is false.

The student is asked for his opinion on statements about the story. This is an open-ended exercise that can be used as the basis for discussion. There are no right or wrong answers.

The beginning of a sentence is supplied, and the student is asked to fill it in with his ideas. If the student claims that he has no feelings about the phrase, the instructor may use substitute phrases. For example, in this particular lesson, substitutions could include "I would (not) want to be president because . . ." or "My favorite president was . . ." The student may need assistance with this exercise, particularly with spelling.

"Good reader . . ." statements emphasize strategies that beginning readers tend to ignore or give students a purpose for an exercise. Many beginning readers do not reread a story to find answers, so this particular statement encourages the student to reread a story in order to do so.

Students are asked to put facts from the story in chronological order. If students have difficulty with this type of exercise, tell them which event came first and let them order the remaining events. Sequencing is an important reading skill.

The directions at the bottom of the page give general guidelines on how to use this page.

★ **Quiz for "Important People: Woodrow Wilson"** ★

A. Write your own title for the story.
   _____

B. From the story, decide if the statements are true. Circle **Yes** or **No**.
   1. Woodrow Wilson always liked school.   Yes   No
   2. Woodrow Wilson liked war.   Yes   No
   3. The people of the world loved Woodrow Wilson. Yes   No
   4. Woodrow Wilson learned to read when he was six. Yes No

C. What do you think?   Circle One
   1. Woodrow Wilson was a good president.   Yes   No   Maybe
   2. Woodrow Wilson had a good mind.   Yes   No   Maybe
   3. Woodrow Wilson loved children.   Yes   No   Maybe

D. Write what you think.
   1. I think Woodrow Wilson _____
      _____
   2. To be president _____
      _____

   | **Good readers** sometimes read a story 2 or 3 times in order to answer questions correctly. |

E. Put the number 1, 2, or 3 next to each sentence to show what happened 1st, 2nd, and 3rd.
   ___ Woodrow Wilson was president of Princeton University.
   ___ Woodrow Wilson learned to read.
   ___ Woodrow Wilson was president of the U.S.A.

(18) Quiz: If necessary, assist the student with exercises A and D. When the student is comfortable with this exercise, similar exercises in later lessons can be assigned as independent work. The answer key is on page 77.

"**Tips on How to Improve Your Reading**" are to be read to the student by the instructor. Tips are designed to deal with the adult beginning reader's concerns about the reading process. Tips discuss many issues, from the usefulness of word families for learning new words to the importance of reading on a consistent basis. The instructor discusses the tips with the student. The instructor and the student can evaluate the tips in terms of their usefulness and discuss strategies for their implementation.

"**Skill Building**" is instructor-assisted, as indicated by the dots. "**Skill Building**" gives the student an opportunity to review old skills and develop new ones. The answers to "**Skill Building**" can be found in the answer key near the back of each book.

The "Good Reader" statements are to be read to the student. They explain why the skills the students are learning are important in the reading process.

The student uses the meaning of a short paragraph to determine which words should be inserted in the blanks. The ability to use the meaning of a sentence to determine word meaning is an important skill for all readers. If the student has difficulty with this exercise, the instructor may write similar exercises, but with only one word missing.

Compound words are built from smaller words that the student already has in his reading vocabulary. The student should read each compound word and circle the smaller words within it.

Using the student's reading vocabulary, words and word parts are combined to form new words. In this lesson, the *all* word family is developed.

Directions explain how this page is to be used.

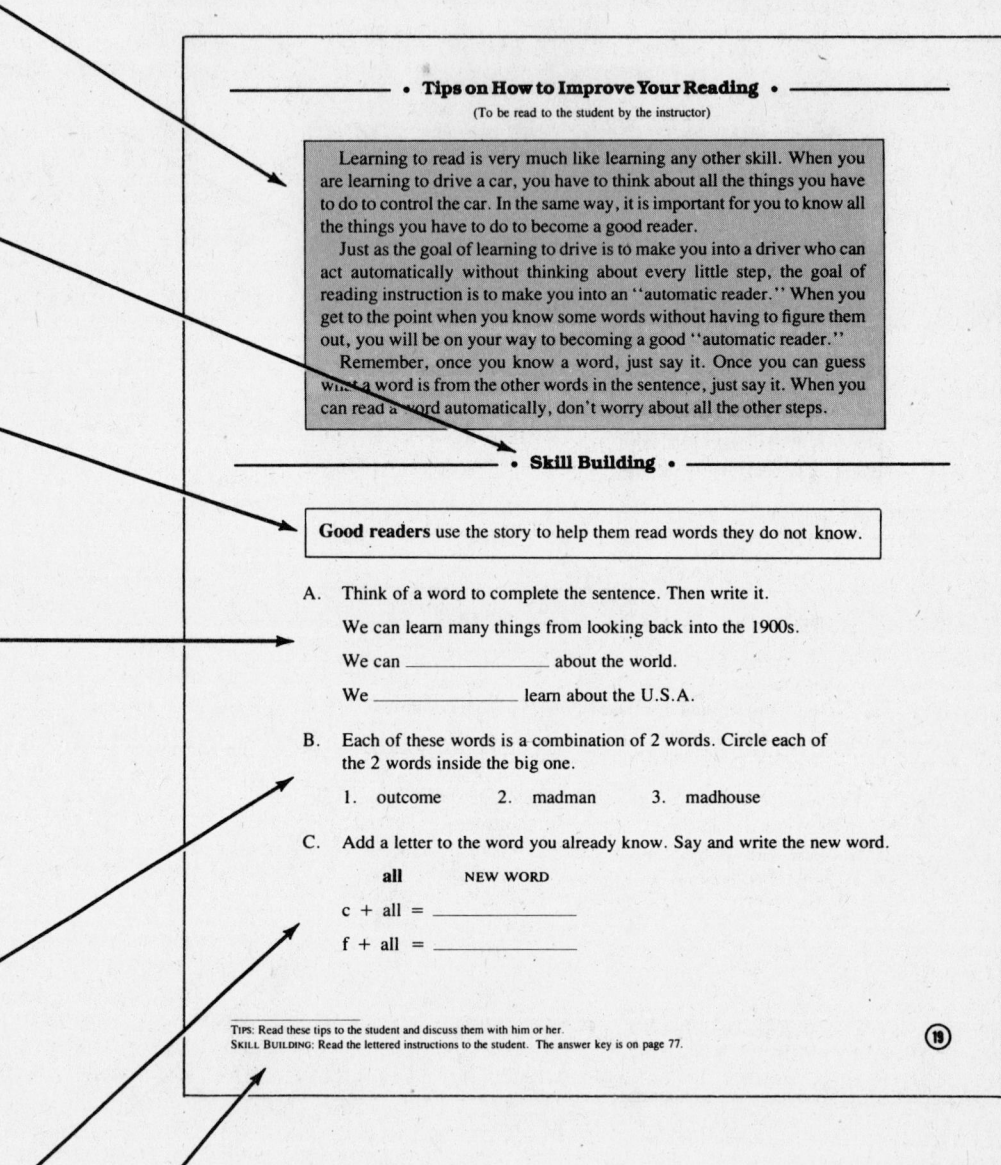

The continuation of the "Skill Building" exercises.

"Good Reader" statements, which are to be read to the student, explain the purpose of the exercise to the student.

Good readers use a word's shape to help them remember the word.

D. Put each word in the shape that fits it.

from
was

E. Read each sentence and write the word that completes it.

president   was   world   made   war   went   from

1. I m ___ him go to school.
2. He w ___ my friend.
3. Do you want to be pr _ _ _ _ _ _ _ ?
4. The quiet girl w ___ to work.
5. We will go fr ___ her house to his house.
6. The w _ _ _ _ is big.
7. Do you want the U.S.A. to go to w ___ ?

F. To learn the **er** ending write the correct word.

1. Pat is old.
   But Dan is _____.
       old older

2. Does the president like
   to _____?
       teach teacher

3. She is little.
   But I think that I am _____.
       little littler

4. Will your baby be
   _____ for me?
       quiet quieter

G. Read the sentences. Then write the words that are in **bold print**.

I do not **mind** your **yelling**. I do not mind your nagging.
I do not mind your being jealous. I **do** mind your spending all the money.

m_____   y_____   d_____

DIRECTIONS: Exercise F shows how er can be added to a word to compare two things.
ADDITIONAL REINFORCEMENT: When the student is comfortable with the new words in this lesson, the flash cards at the end of the book can be used for reinforcement.

(20)

Students are asked to look at the shape of a word and then place it in the correct set of boxes. This can serve as a memory aid for many beginning students.

The student is asked to use the meaning of a sentence to determine which word goes in the blank. This exercise uses all of the new words from this lesson so that the student has a chance to practice these new vocabulary words.

Learning how to use the meaning of a sentence to determine an unfamiliar word is very useful for beginning readers. Using sentence meaning is one of the basic methods that a reader uses to figure out an unfamiliar word.

The **-er** ending is taught by asking the student to select the correct word for each sentence. This gives the student another tool for working with unknown words.

Words from previous lessons are reviewed. After reading the short paragraph, the student writes the words that are in bold print.

Directions are included at the bottom of the page. These directions remind the instructor that flash cards for the new words from this lesson are available at the back of the book.

The stars on either side of the title indicate that this page can be assigned for independent work if the student is capable of doing it on his own.

In the even-numbered books, "**Reading to Know Others**" focuses on one person's narrative. The person usually discusses some aspect of the topic presented in that lesson.

Open-ended questions frequently follow the reading. These can be used as a basis for a discussion on the topic of the lesson.

Directions at the bottom of the page give general guidelines on how to use this page.

★ **Reading to Know Others** ★

Manny writes:

That Woodrow Wilson was something. I think that he was a good teacher. Maybe he was a good president too.

But how did he go from being a teacher to being president? Little kids may think about being president. But not as they become older. Does a man become president for the money? Or maybe he wants to be the most important man in the U.S.A? As for me, I do not want to be president of the U.S.A. I do not want to work all the time.

But does the president have to work all of the time? Maybe he does. Maybe he does not. Many people work for the president. He can tell other people what to do. He can work if he wants to work. But he does not have to work.

I am good at telling other people what to do. The people at work say I am a good boss. Sometimes my kids say that I am a nag. But they do what I tell them.

The more I think about it, the more I want to be president. Maybe I will be president at some time.

WHAT DO YOU THINK?

Do you think the president works all the time?

Do you want to be president?

READING TO KNOW OTHERS: This exercise can be assigned for independent work.
REMINDER: Flash cards for the new words are located at the end of the book and can be used at the instructor's discretion.

• Time to Write •

Look at the sample time line on the left and then fill in your own on the right.

	1985	I go back to school.	1985
	1980	I have a baby.	1980
		I am married.	
		I go to work.	
Vietnam War	1970		1970
	1960		1960
		I have a baby brother.	
		I go to school.	
Korean War	1950		1950
		I am a baby.	
World War 2	1940	My Dad goes to war.	1940
The Depression	1930		1930
		My Dad goes to school.	
	1920	My Dad is a baby.	1920

DIRECTIONS: Read the instructions to the students. Encourage the students to fill in their own time lines, but assist them with spelling any words that they need help with. Reassure any student who has difficulty with the exercise that copying the model word for word is quite appropriate.

(22)

Dots around the title indicate that **"Time to Write"** is an instructor-assisted activity.

"Time to Write" is a structured language-experience activity. In **"Time to Write,"** the student reads an example of something that another person has written. In this lesson there are two time lines: one indicates major historical events, and the other is used to record important events in the student's life. This exercise will give the student some sense of how personal events relate to historical events.

The instructor should assist the student with spelling any words that the student needs help with. In the earlier books, if the student has difficulty generating ideas, the student may copy the model word for word. If the student has difficulty writing, he may dictate his thoughts to the instructor. The instructor should write the student's thoughts on a separate piece of paper and then let the student copy them into the book. Students who dictate their writings should be encouraged to begin writing on their own as they move through later books in *New Beginnings*.

The directions at the bottom of the page give the instructor suggestions on how to present this activity to the student.

50 NEW BEGINNINGS IN READING: INSTRUCTOR'S GUIDE

Dots around the title indicate that "**Sounding It Out**" is an instructor-assisted activity.

A picture cue is provided to help the student remember the sound being taught. This lesson covers the short **i** sound. The instructor may want to review the word with the student so that the student will remember the sound and the cue.

The student is asked to circle the pictures of words beginning with the sound that is covered in this lesson.

The student looks at each of the pictures and puts the correct letter in the blank to complete the new word.

The student reads two sentences that have new words based on the sound covered in this lesson.

The student selects the correct word to complete the sentence. This exercise reinforces words with the sound that is covered in this lesson.

The student is asked to identify and circle the words with the sound taught in this lesson.

Directions at the bottom of the page give the instructor general guidelines on how these activities should be carried out.

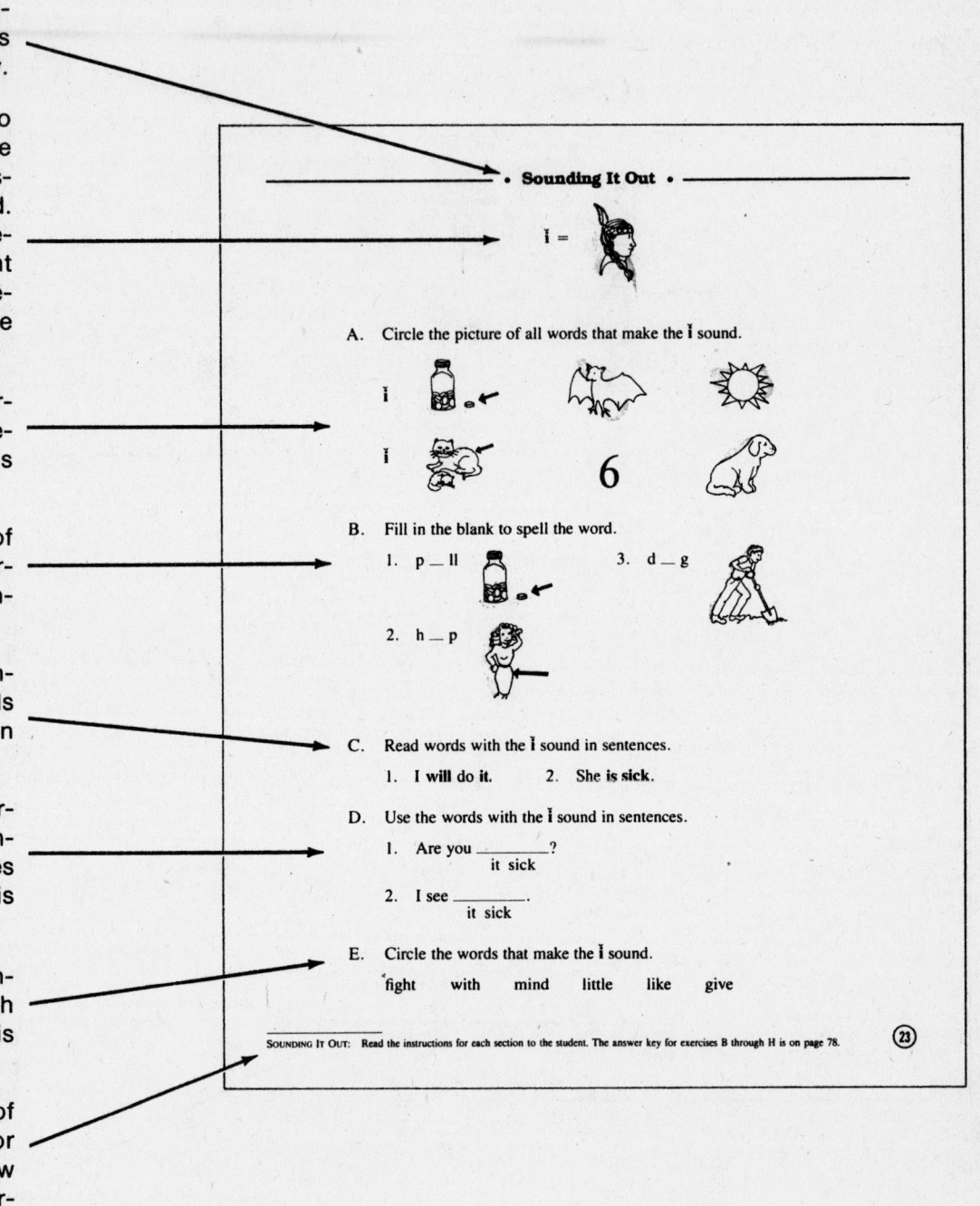

The continuation of the "Sounding It Out" activities.

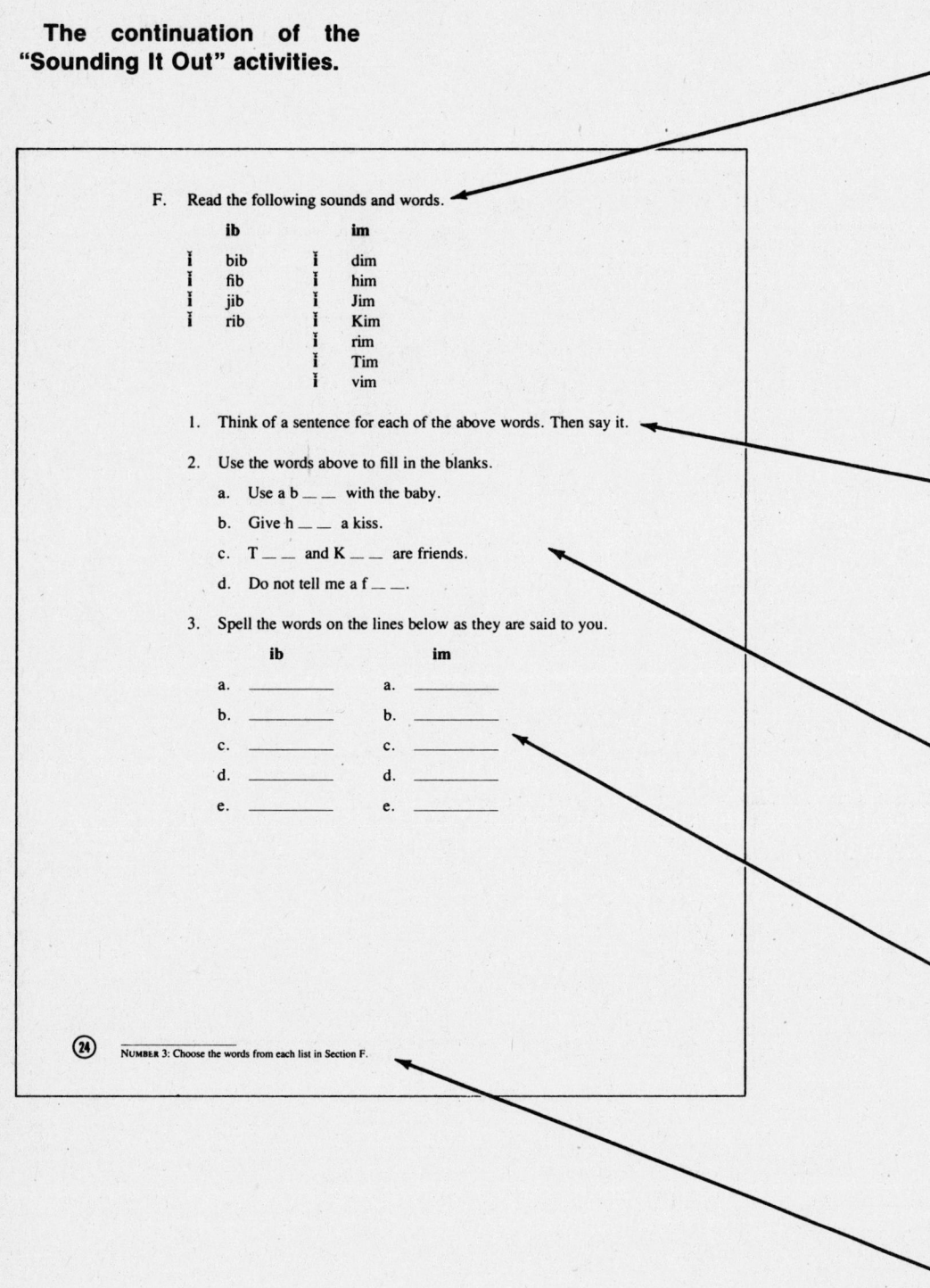

In each **"Sounding It Out"** exercise, word families (rhyming words) are presented that use the sound being covered in the lesson. The word families have three purposes: (1) they reinforce the sounds that are presented in that lesson, (2) they give the student an effective tool in identifying unknown words, and (3) they increase the student's reading vocabulary in a painless, efficient manner.

The word families are reinforced by having the student think of a sentence for the words in each word family. To make the activity more challenging, the instructor may ask the student to incorporate more than one word from a family in a sentence.

The words in each word family are reinforced when the student fills in the blank with the correct word.

This exercise may be handled in two different ways. For students who are highly motivated to learn to spell, this exercise may be conducted as a spelling test. For students who are not inclined toward spelling, the instructor can read each word in the word families. The student can either find and copy the word or attempt to spell the word without referring to the list.

The directions remind the instructor that the spelling words should be taken from the word list at the top of the page.

The conclusion of the "Sounding It Out" activities.

To reinforce the words in the word families that were just taught, the student looks at the picture and reads the three sentences, selecting the sentence that best describes the picture.

The student writes the word that best describes each picture. If the student has any difficulty with this, he should be encouraged to look back at the earlier exercises, either to find the word that best describes the picture or to check the spelling of the word.

The student is given the opportunity to evaluate his performance in **"Sounding It Out."** The instructor should remember that students need a large amount of positive reinforcement, even if their performance was less than perfect. Emphasize the ways that the student is improving as a reader.

The directions indicate that an answer key can be found near the back of the book.

While this lesson gives the general format of the **"Sounding It Out"** exercises, the instructor should be aware that the phonics exercises in later books do contain several variations.

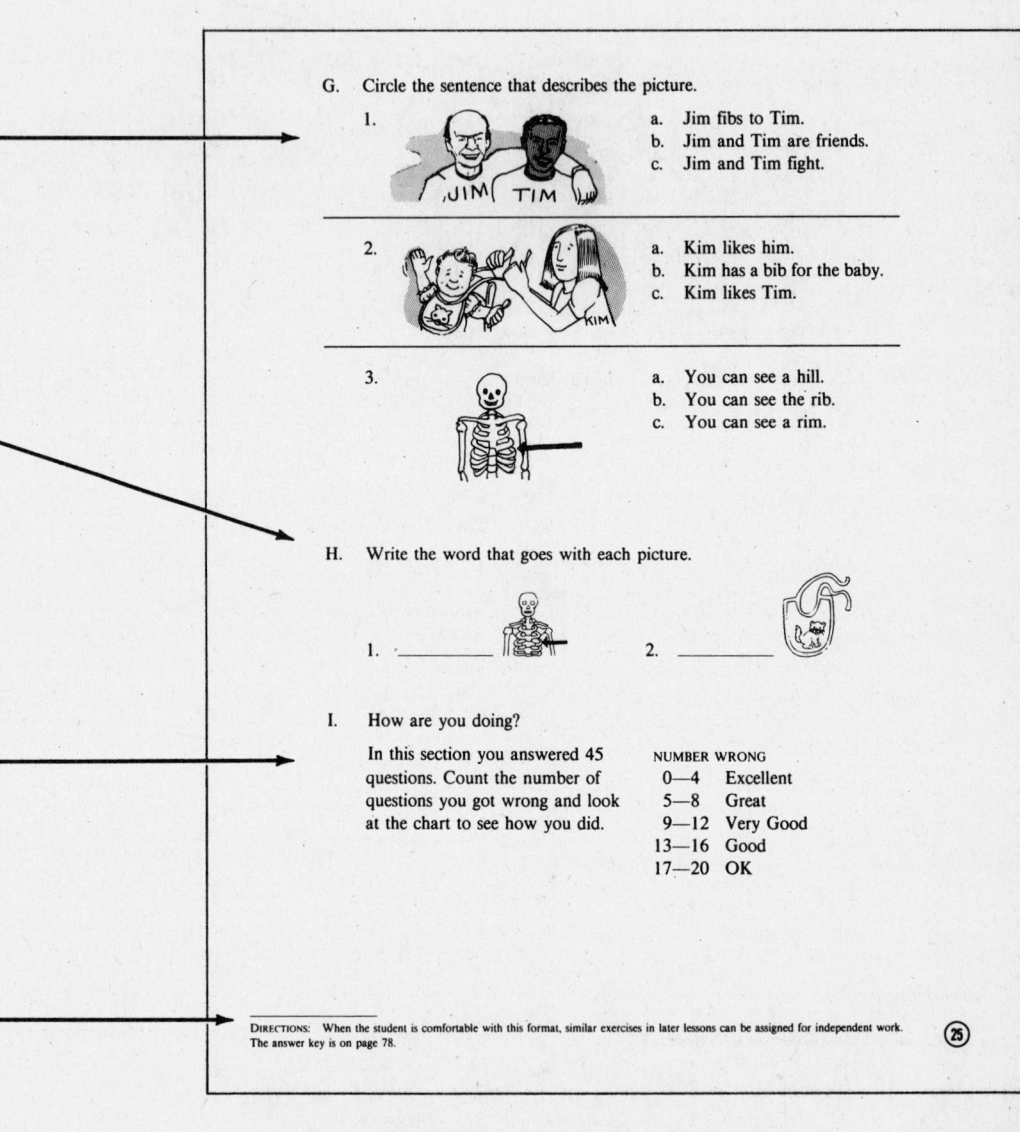

ON YOUR OWN

★ Know Your Presidents ★

All of the presidents were important. They said and did important things. But they were people too. In many ways they were like you and me. They had families. They worked. They had friends. And sometimes they did not have all the things that they wanted.

Read about 3 presidents and the things they did. Read about who they were as people.

George Washington
President from 1789 to 1797

George Washington was married to Martha Washington. But they did not have children. He liked being president. But he did not love being president.

We will be a free people.

Abraham Lincoln
President from 1861 to 1865

Abraham Lincoln was married and had 4 boys. 1 of the boys was killed in the war. Mrs. Lincoln was always jealous. But when her boy was killed, she went mad.

All people will be free.

Franklin Roosevelt
President from 1933 to 1945

Franklin Roosevelt's family had money. But Franklin was sickly as a child. And he was sickly when he was president.

Children, people with no money, old people, workers without work, all are important.

DIRECTIONS: This page reinforces the skills and vocabulary words presented in this lesson. When the student is familiar with this format, these exercises can be assigned for independent work.

It is strongly suggested that the "**On Your Own**" activities be assigned for independent work. The "**On Your Own**" exercises usually consist of the last three to five pages of each lesson. While students should be encouraged to do the activities on their own, the instructor may want to follow up these activities by discussing the stories with the students.

The "**On Your Own**" activities vary from book to book, but the exercises within each book follow a similar format from lesson to lesson.

Each lesson contains several short readings. This reading briefly describes the personal lives and political philosophy of three presidents. Students may need some assistance in reading the names of the presidents. Instructors may want to use these readings as a basis for discussion.

The directions in the "**On Your Own**" exercises suggest that these exercises be assigned as independent work as soon as the student is able to handle them by himself.

It is suggested that "**On Your Own**" activities be assigned as independent work as soon as the student is able to do the work on his own.

"**Playing with Words**" contains several fun activities that are designed to reinforce the vocabulary words from this and previous lessons.

This activity reinforces the new words from each lesson by presenting them in a sentence and then in the word finds. This is usually one of the most popular activities in each lesson, as it is invariably a successful experience for the student.

The student is directed to put the scrambled words into a sequence that forms sentences. If a student experiences difficulty, the instructor should place all but two or three of the words in their proper sequence. As the student works through *New Beginnings*, the instructor should give less and less assistance on this type of exercise, until the student can do it without any assistance.

The students are asked to write their own tongue twisters using all of the words that have been taught that begin with a specific letter. Students should be encouraged to write rough drafts of their own tongue twisters before writing them into the book.

The directions indicate that the answer key for "**Playing with Words**" is located near the back of the book.

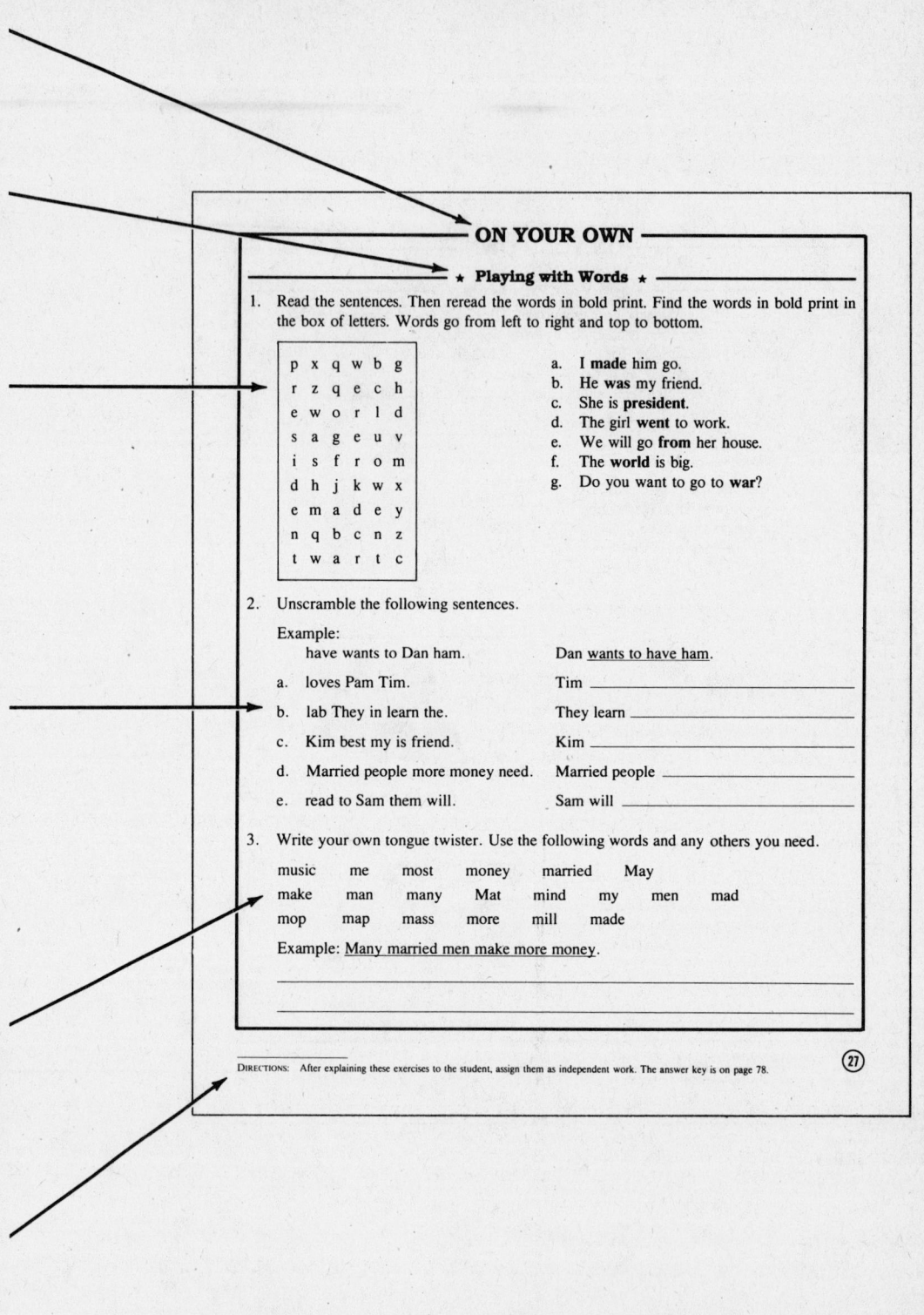

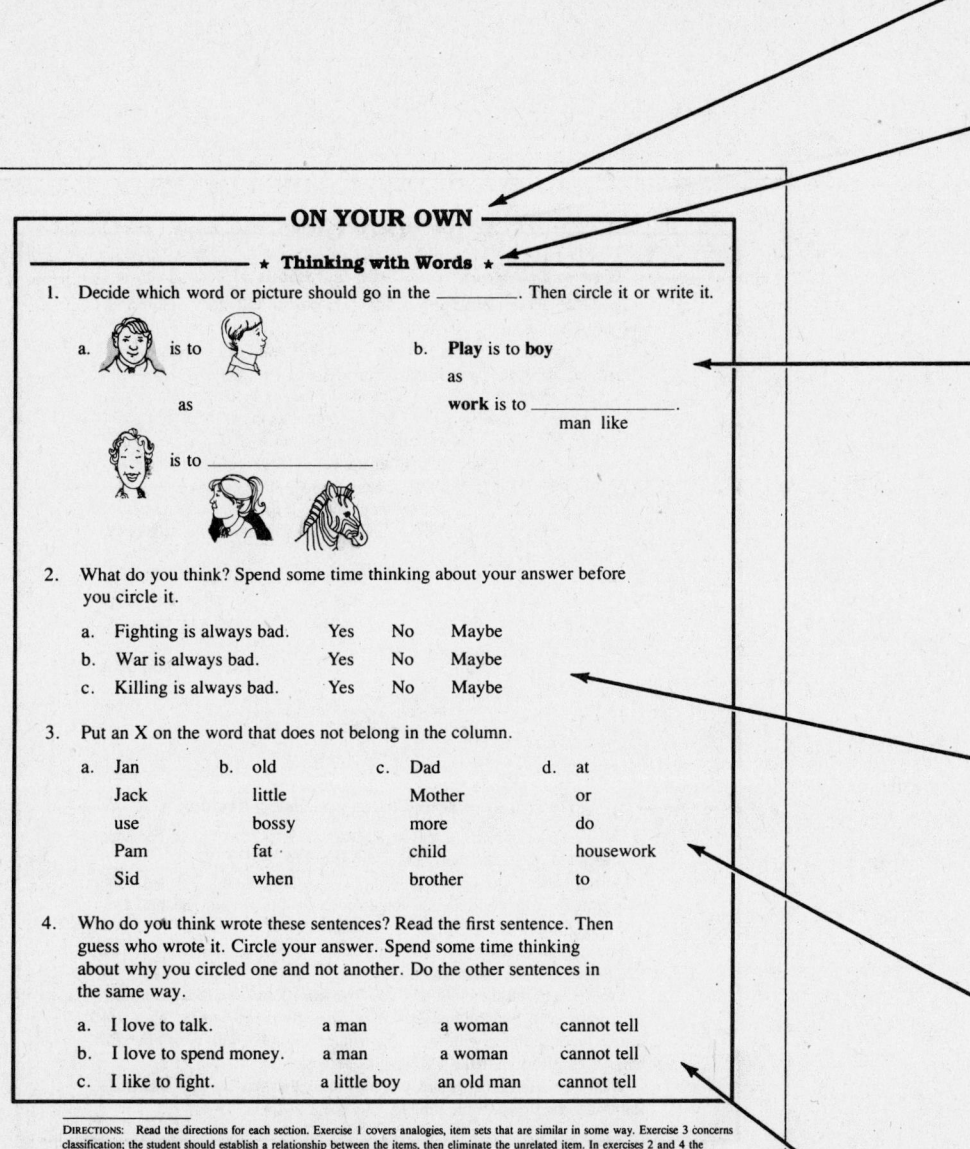

"**On Your Own**" can be assigned as independent work as soon as the student is able to do the work on his own.

"**Thinking with Words**" consists of four exercises that give the student an opportunity to engage in higher-level thinking skills.

The student is asked to complete two analogies—item sets that are similar in some way. The first analogy is shown using pictures, while the second one relies on words. Initially, some students may need an explanation of analogies, with several oral examples (*yes* is to *no* as *up* is to _____, or *shoe* is to *foot* as *mitten* is to _____).

The student is directed to make value judgments about three statements. These statements may be used as a basis for discussion. There are no right or wrong answers in this activity—although some of the discussions may be fairly heated!

The student is asked to look at each of the lists of words and determine which word does not belong in a list. For example, in the list that reads, *Jan*, *Jack*, *use*, *Pam*, and *Sid*, the word *use* is eliminated since it is the only word that is not a person's name.

The student is asked to read three statements and decide who made that statement. This activity can serve as the basis for discussing the assumptions that the student brings with him.

Directions at the bottom of the page describe the purpose of each activity.

The "**On Your Own**" activities should be assigned as independent work.

The instructor may want to discuss the readings with the student after the student has read the stories. In this particular activity, the stories can serve as the basis for a discussion on child rearing practices. Possible questions to discuss are: What is the best way to deal with children when they fight? How did your parents deal with you? How do you deal with your children?

Directions at the bottom of the page give general guidelines on how to use this page.

ON YOUR OWN

★ How to Tell When Your Child Is Jealous of Your Baby ★

People do not think that little children are jealous. But many children are jealous of babies.

It is important to know if your child is jealous. Then you can do something about it. Look for 3 things to see if your child is jealous.

A child may think that he has to be like a baby to be loved. He may talk baby talk. He may ask for a bib. If he does baby-like things, he is telling you something. He thinks you want the baby, not him.

Sometimes a child will be mad at the baby. He thinks the baby is too important to you. He thinks, "They have the baby. They do not want me." The child may ask you to give the baby away. If he tells you that he does not like the baby, he is telling you something. He thinks you want the baby, not him.

The little child who thinks that you do not love him may be sad. He may be quiet. He may not play the way he used to play. The child who always looks sad is telling you something, too. He thinks that you want the baby, not him.

If you think your child is jealous, read "How to Free Your Child from Being Jealous."

★ How to Free Your Child from Being Jealous ★

Many times a little child will be jealous of a baby. Your child becomes jealous when he thinks that you do not love him.

With a baby in the house, you have many things to do. You may not have time for your child. When you do not have time for him, he thinks he is not important. He thinks he is not wanted.

You may have made the child jealous with the things you did. You can free the child from being jealous.

You have to tell the child that you love him. You have to tell him that he is important. But children learn best from the things you do. You will have to make him see your love. You will have to play with him. You will have to read to him. You will have to be with him.

With 2 children in the house, you may think that you cannot make time. But you have to make the time to love the **2** of them.

Two Reading Exercises: These exercises provide reinforcement and can be assigned as independent work.

Extra Features: Pretests, Flash Cards, More Reading, Getting Ready, Posttest, Certificate of Mastery, Answer Key, and Word Lists

Pretests are presented at the beginning of each book in *New Beginnings* and are to be used with students who have not taken the *Placement Test*. The **pretest** will indicate whether that particular book is an appropriate place for the student to begin work.

If, for some reason, a student cannot be tested and the instructor has a strong sense of the student's reading vocabulary, the **word list** at the back of any book can be used to determine the appropriate book in which to begin.

If you have just started working with a student and the *Placement Test* is not available, you should administer the **pretest** in *Groundbreaker Exercises*, and then, if necessary, administer the **pretests** in the following books until the proper level is found.

The directions at the bottom of each **pretest** page list the criteria for placement in a particular book. **Pretests** in all of the books have two parts: a reading section and a phonics section.

The readings, which are oriented toward adults, contain all the sight words presented in their respective books.

The phonics sections of each **pretest** contain the phonics principles presented in that particular book.

Book 2 Pretest
(35 sight words and short i)

EXERCISE 1:   Read this letter.

Jan. 3, 1942

To my baby girl,

You are my first child. And I want to tell you many, many things. About me. About your mother. About why we had you. And about the way I feel about you.

At first I was afraid of you. I did not know what you wanted or what to do for you. You and your mother were good teachers. But I learned slowly.

But then you went from being a baby to being a little girl. We played. You sat on my lap. I read to you. We made things.

And you used to come to me and ask me to tell you a story. But you did not want one story. You always wanted more and more. But I have no more time for stories. And I have some important things to say to you.

I have to go to war. And I may or may not come back. When you are an adult, you will read what I wrote. And as an adult I want to tell you some things.

I believe that a woman can do anything she wants to do. If she wants to get married that is OK, but she can do other things too. If you want to be president, you can do it. If you want to write books, do it. Live the way you want to live. Be who you want to be. The world can be a good place.

I will always love you,

Dad

EXERCISE 2:   Say these sounds.

ig   ip   ick   it   id   ill   im   in   ib   ix   iss

PRETEST DIRECTIONS: Read the instructions to the student. If a student misses six or more words or appears to be frustrated, discontinue the pretest. After explaining that these words will be taught in Book 2, proceed to Exercise 2. Record the short vowel sounds that the student has difficulty with. If a student misses 6 or more words, begin work in Lesson 1. If the student misses fewer than six words, teach him or her the words and short vowel sounds missed and then proceed to the pretest in Book 3.

v

The directions at the bottom of the page include the criteria that will indicate whether the student should enter this particular book or proceed to a higher book for additional testing.

Flash cards are available at the back of each book for all of the sight words presented in that particular book. After the student has been introduced to the new words in each lesson, the instructor may want to use the **flash cards** with the student for additional reinforcement.

After the student has completed a lesson, cut out the **flash cards** for that lesson. Show the student the side of the card that has only the word and have him read the words. Separate the words that he misreads from the words he reads correctly. The student should be instructed to use the picture and the sentence on the back of the card as a memory aid for the word. If the student can generate any other pictures that will act as a cue they should also be put on the back of the card.

If it is possible, number the cards that the student reads incorrectly and record them on a cassette tape. On the tape, read the number of the card, and then wait five seconds before reading the word on the card. The student should be instructed to try reading the card in that five-second interval and compare it to the instructor's reading.

Some students have difficulty with **flash cards**. A warning against using flash cards with all students and instructions on how to use them are listed at the bottom of the page.

afraid	feel	woman	adult	slow	on
ask	first	any	that	place	believe
get	mother	one	live	story	why

WARNING: Some students have great difficulty reading one word at a time. If this is true for your student, discontinue the use of flash cards. Many people learn to read well without flash cards.

INSTRUCTIONS FOR USE OF FLASH CARDS: After the student has completed a lesson, cut out the flash cards for that lesson. Show the student the side of the card that has only the word. Separate those words he or she misreads from those words that he or she reads correctly. The student should be instructed to use the picture and sentence on the back of the card as a memory aid for the word.

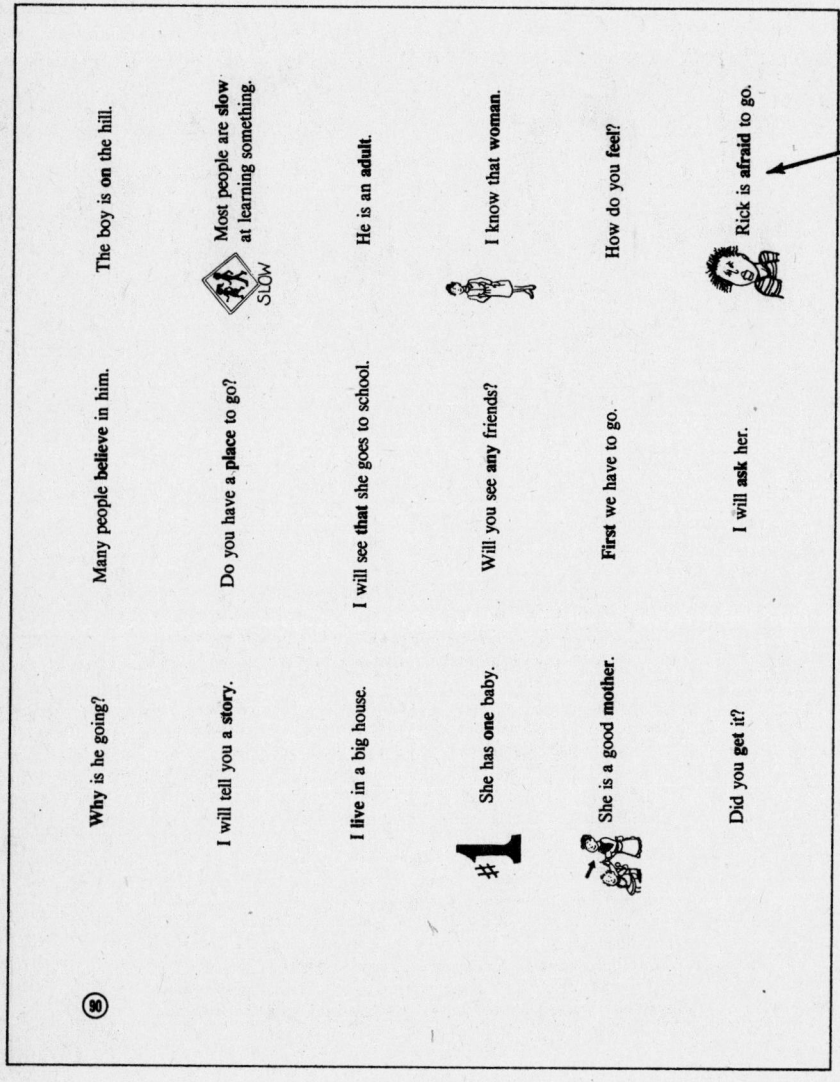

Many **flash cards** have a picture cue and all use the word in a sentence so that the student can use these as aids if he needs a reminder.

Beginning in *Book 2*, there is a series of stories about Dan and Jane, and their life together. These stories are presented at the end of the lessons in each book in a section called **More Readings.** It is recommended that these be assigned for independent work after the student has completed the lessons in each book. Although the stories are interrelated, each can stand on its own.

The stories start with Dan and Jane in high school. They meet and fall in love. They are married, and experience the ups and downs of married life. They raise a family. Divorce is a threat, but they work out their differences.

The stories should be used to emphasize the student's increased reading competence.

★ **The Bookmans** ★

ANN

I am married to Will and we have one child. Dan, my boy, is 14. Will works at the high school. He fixes things. He likes his work. Sometimes I work.

We wanted to have more children. I wanted to have a little girl. But I was older when we married.

I did not work before I married. I lived with my mother. She was sickly. I did things for her. I read to her. I made her jam. I wrote to people for her. I did all the housework.

When I was little, my mother was good to me. She was a good woman in other ways, too. I loved her and liked her. She did not get to see Dan. I feel bad about that. She passed away before I married Will.

Dan is a good boy. Like his Dad, he is quiet. He likes to fix things. But he is like me in some ways, too. People say he looks like me. I love music and he loves music. He is learning how to play the sax.

WILL

I work in the high school. It is a good place to work. I like the kids and the teachers. The other six workers are good people, too.

I do not have money. But I have the important things. I have good friends. I have work that I like. I am married, and I have a child.

I married 2 times. The first woman I married was a nag. All she wanted was money. But she did not work. She wanted me to give her things.

Advanced Phonics Exercises

Lesson 3

A. Read each of the following words. The words that are marked by an asterisk are nonsense words.

pit	hit	bit	lid	did	pick	sick
wit	fit	kit	hid	kid	kick	tick
sit	lit	* dit	bid	rid	Rick	lick
it	* rit		Sid	* id	* ick	Nick

B. Review the ă word families.

cab	gab	bat	fat	mat	cap
jab	tab	rat	cat	pat	lap
lab	* zab	sat	hat	* zat	rap
nab		at	* wat		

C. Apply what you know about word families to longer words.

vis it	Will you **visit** me?
rap id	He ran **rapidly**.
pic nic	Do you want to go on a **picnic**?
rab bit	The child has a **rabbit**.
tim id	She is **timid**.
at tic	What is in the **attic**?

Lesson 4

A. Read each of the following words. The words that are marked by an asterisk are nonsense words.

pin	* zin	him	dim	pill	fill	ill	rid
win	in	rim	* bim	will	kill	Jill	Sid
tin	kin	Tim		bill	hill	mill	* id
fin		* lim		* nill	* zill	* rill	

PURPOSE: The Advanced Phonics Exercises are for students who completed Sounding It Out without difficulty. They show the student how to decode words that are phonically regular. The Advanced Phonics Exercises are correlated to Lessons 3, 4, and 5.
DIRECTIONS: Explain the purpose of this exercise and inform the student that nonsense words will be used to see how well he or she has learned the word families in the previous lessons. The nonsense words have asterisks next to them.

"**Advanced Phonics Exercises**" are to be used with students who have little difficulty with "**Sounding It Out**." They are correlated with Lessons 3, 4, and 5. The purpose of the **advanced phonics exercises** is to show students how to decode words that are phonically regular.

Nonsense words are presented within the context of word families, in order to make them easier for the student.

"**Getting Ready**" prepares the student to take the **posttest** by giving him additional practice on the sight words presented in each lesson in that particular book. The vast majority of students enjoy word finds.

The instructor should read the instructions to the student and emphasize that the student should seek help for any words that he is unsure of.

Getting Ready

You can use the words and word finds below to prepare for the posttest. You can do this by reading the words before you find them. If you cannot read a word, go to the lesson where it is introduced or ask your instructor to help you. Remember that the words in the word find go from left to right and from top to bottom.

Lesson 1

w	h	o	m	x	c
a	g	o	o	d	o
y	z	f	r	o	m
x	o	r	e	r	e

come   who
way   of
or   more
good

Lesson 2

z	q	x	w	e	n	t	z	g
b	u	f	w	e	r	e	b	h
c	v	r	a	w	a	r	c	j
g	x	o	s	m	a	d	e	k
h	y	m	w	o	r	l	d	q
p	r	e	s	i	d	e	n	t

president   was
were   went
world   from
made   war

Lesson 3

b	w	h	y	w	f	j
o	s	t	o	r	y	k
o	a	x	n	i	g	m
k	y	z	c	t	h	q
b	e	l	i	e	v	e

book   story
on   believe
write   why
say

Lesson 4

a	d	u	l	t
s	l	o	w	h
x	i	n	a	a
z	v	e	n	t
g	e	f	y	r
p	l	a	c	e

one   adult
that   place
live   any
slow

Lesson 5

b	x	f	e	e	l
c	z	i	g	e	t
a	f	r	a	i	d
j	a	s	k	x	y
m	o	t	h	e	r
p	w	o	m	a	n

woman   ask
feel   afraid
mother   first
get

GETTING READY: Read the instructions to the student and assist him or her with any words that he or she cannot read.

The **posttest** serves two purposes. It should be used to emphasize the student's increased competence with the words and skills presented in that book. Even if a student experiences some difficulty in the **posttest**, point out all the material that has been mastered. The second purpose of the **posttest** is to give the instructor an opportunity to evaluate the student's progress.

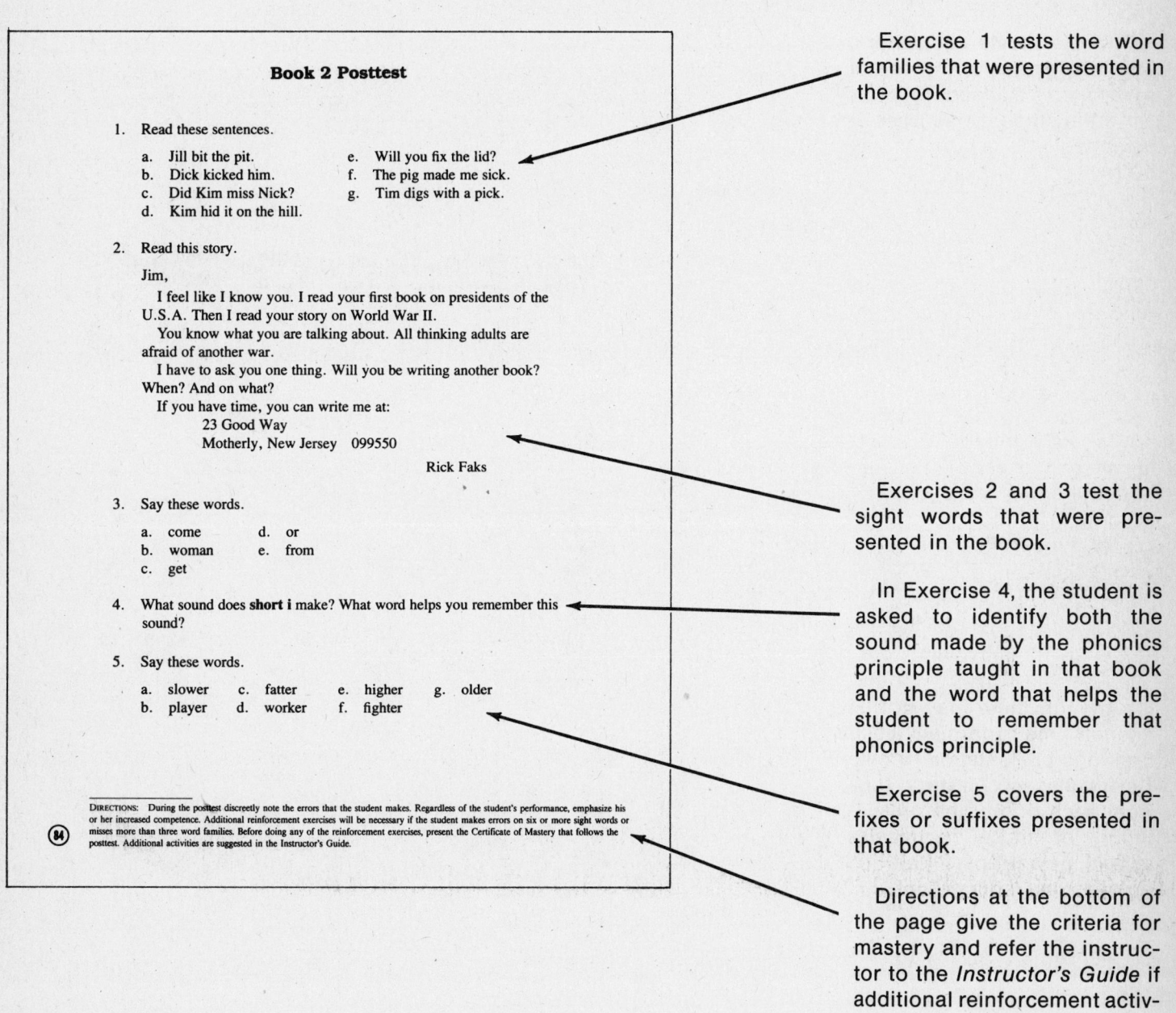

Exercise 1 tests the word families that were presented in the book.

Exercises 2 and 3 test the sight words that were presented in the book.

In Exercise 4, the student is asked to identify both the sound made by the phonics principle taught in that book and the word that helps the student to remember that phonics principle.

Exercise 5 covers the prefixes or suffixes presented in that book.

Directions at the bottom of the page give the criteria for mastery and refer the instructor to the *Instructor's Guide* if additional reinforcement activities seem necessary.

The **Certificate of Mastery**, which is located at the end of each book, is used to celebrate the student's success in completing the material in that book.

It is suggested that the **Certificate of Mastery** be removed from the book, and the blanks filled in, prior to the presentation of the certificate.

Although there may not be enough time to formally celebrate the presentation of nine **Certificates of Mastery** (one from each book), the presentation of these certificates should be set apart from the normal classroom routine.

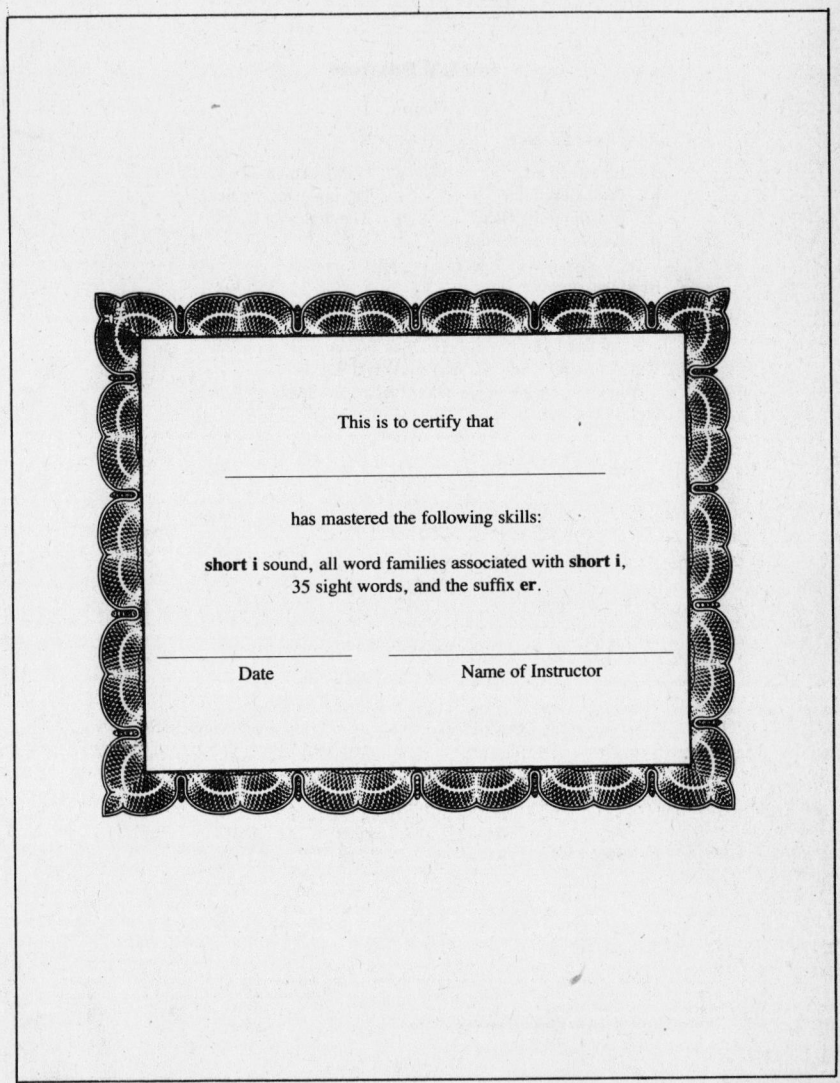

Sample Lessons—Extra Features 65

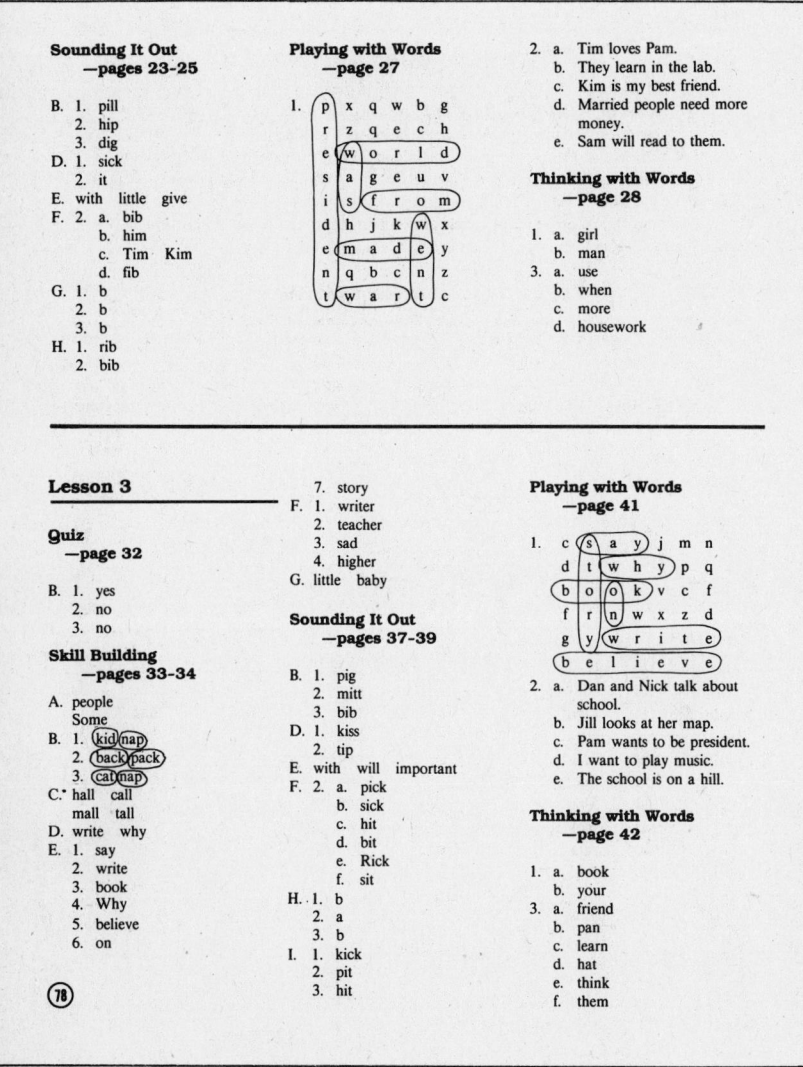

An "**Answer Key**" is available for all exercises and activities that have a correct answer. Open-ended activities are not included.

Each lesson includes several notations at the bottom of the page that indicate where the answer keys can be found. There are also notations on the answer key page that indicate where the answers come from. When the student is comfortable with the format of the **Answer Key**, the student should take the responsibility for correcting his own work.

The **Word List** includes all the sight words and word families taught in that particular book, as well as the sight words from the previous books.

The directions explain the ways that the word lists can be used.

Word List

Uses of Word List: The Word List has three basic uses. 1) For students who resist testing, the Word List can be used to determine whether or not Book 2 is appropriate for the student. 2) Prior to assigning independent work in Book 2, the instructor can examine the Word List to ensure that the student knows a high percentage of the words. 3) The instructor can use the Word List as a resource for creating additional reinforcement activities.

Groundbreaker Exercises

Lesson 1	Lesson 2	Lesson 3	Lesson 4	Lesson 5	Lesson 6	Lesson 7
love	house	play	boy	talk	they	quiet
work	school	music	girl	fight	are	people
like	time	friend	child	old	money	jealous
do	think	for	children	me	yell	most
does	read	thing	the	he	married	may
not	go	have	is	will	about	look
he	to	see	can	she	with	make
you	too		want			

Book 1

Lesson 1

and	bat	ban
family	cat	can
some	fat	Dan
all	hat	fan
little	mat	Jan
we	pat	man
tell	rat	Nan
	sat	pan
	that	ran
		tan

Lesson 2

how	gal	bag
mind	Hal	gag
be	pal	hag
know	Sal	lag
then		nag
waste		rag
high		tag
		wag

Lesson 3

boss	bad	ax
bossy	dad	Max
important	had	tax
men	lad	wax
teach	mad	
teacher	pad	
my	sad	
best		
use		

Suggestions for Teaching Sight Words and Phonics

There are many suggestions for teaching sight words and phonics throughout this instructor's guide, but for the instructor's convenience, they are also grouped together here for easy reference.

Sight Words

If the student has difficulty with some of the new words in a lesson, the instructor may want to try one, or several, of the following.
1. After the new word has been identified, ask the student to look at the word and say it in a sentence.
2. Ask the student to write the word that is posing problems, while saying it.
3. Ask the student to use the initial or consonant sounds, phonics patterns, or word families that she knows to identify the new word.
4. Have the student read the word in another context. The instructor could write sentences that include the new word. Emotionally charged or incongruous sentences can usually serve as a memory aid for the student.
5. Direct the student to write out the new word until she can spell it from memory.
6. Work with the student using the flash cards at the back of the book. Specific instructions for working with the flash cards can be found on pages 58–59 of this manual.
7. If the student has difficulty mastering the new words, the second page of the lesson can be used for additional reinforcement.

    In the odd-numbered books, the second page of the lesson contains pictured words that can serve as a cue for some of the new words, and a play where the new words are usually introduced in the instructor's role.

    In the even-numbered books, the second page of the lesson has a reading that contains all of the new words. If the student has not mastered the new words on the first page, the instructor should read the passage to the student several times, with the student following along in her book. The instructor and the student should then read the selection together. When you read with the student, you may start to say words just before the student says them. This can be extremely useful to the student. By starting to say the word just before the student says it, you are providing the student with a strong cue as to what the word is. This discrepancy occurs naturally because the student is a hesitant reader, while the instructor is confident. After reading the passage together several times, the student should then read it independently.
8. If a student continues to have difficulty learning words, provide as much high-interest repetition of these words as possible. If the student enjoys word finds, make up word finds for her. If a student likes to unscramble sentences, provide her with scrambled sentences. The point is to provide the student with repetition that is interesting.

Phonics

If a student has difficulty mastering a phonics principle, the instructor may find the following suggestions useful.
1. Write the letter (or letter combination) that the student is studying and give her an example of a word that starts with that sound, such as the **a** in *astronaut*. Then generate a list of

---

NOTE: To avoid sexist language, we have alternated male and female pronouns in this book. All references to instructors and students pertain to both sexes except when a specific person is being discussed.

words that begin with the **a** sound.
2. Make sure that the student can discriminate the sound that she is learning. For example, if the student is learning the short **a** sound, say the short **a** sound for her and then ask if she can hear it in the word *apple*. Then ask if that sound is in the word *egg*, and several other words, until it is clear that the student can discriminate the sound correctly.

There are students who are not, and may never be, ready for phonics. For some students, this is an inappropriate method for learning to read. If your student has *great* difficulty discriminating and producing sounds and is unable to complete the phonics work in the lessons, discontinue the phonics work in **"Sounding It Out"** and concentrate on the word families.

3. Have the student select her own guide word (cue word) for the phonics principle being presented or use the guide word provided by the book. Periodically, ask the student to say the sound that she has learned and the guide word.
4. If a student needs additional reinforcement beyond the phonics work included in New Beginnings, the instructor may want to purchase a phonics workbook (see Supplemental Materials, page 69).

Phonics Pages in New Beginnings

Sounds	Where to Find Work on the Sounds
all consonant sounds	Groundbreaker, pp. 7, 14, 28, 50–71
short **a** sound	Book 1, pp. 8–10, 23–25, 38–40, 53–55, 68–70
short **i** sound	Book 2, pp. 8–10, 23–25, 37–39, 51–53, 64–66
short **u** sound	Book 3, pp. 8–10, 21–23, 35–37, 48–50, 62–64
short **o** sound	Book 4, pp. 8–10, 22–24, 35–37, 48–50, 61–63
short **e** sound	Book 5, pp. 8–10, 21–23, 34–36, 47–49, 60–62
all long vowels	Book 6, pp. 8–10, 22–24, 36–38, 50–52, 63–65
bl, cl, fl, gl, pl, sl	Book 7, pp. 8–10, 21–23, 65–66
fr, gr, pr, tr, br, cr, dr	Book 7, pp. 36–38, 50–52, 65–66
th, wh, ch, sh	Book 8, pp. 8–10, 21–23, 35–37, 49–51, 62–64

Supplemental Materials

These materials will provide students with supplementary work and readings for *New Beginnings in Reading*.

PHONICS WORKBOOKS

Elwell, Clarence. *Phonics Workbooks*, Levels A–C. Cleveland: Modern Curriculum Press, 1976.

Ervin, J. *Phonics Workbook*, Level D. Cleveland: Modern Curriculum Press, 1977.

These four workbooks cover the basic phonics skills.

Hall, N., and Price, R. *Explode the Code*. Cambridge, Mass.: Educators Publishing Service, Inc., 1976.

Eight workbooks that cover the basic phonics skills. The books are well paced and follow a logical sequence.

SUPPLEMENTAL READING FOR STUDENTS

The following books have been listed according to the vocabulary demands placed on the student. These books should be read in the order in which they appear.

Keller, R. *Two for the Road*. Syracuse: New Readers Press, 1979.

This is a very short story about a woman trucker and the man who tries to dominate her. The feminist orientation is difficult for some students, but the limited vocabulary and adult theme make this book a winner.

McFall, K. *Pat King's Family*. Syracuse: New Readers Press, 1977.

Nicely done story about a young woman who has been abandoned by her husband. Although the subject sounds depressing, this is an upbeat book with very nice pictures and a limited vocabulary.

People. New York: Educational Developmental Laboratories, 1977.

A collection of thirty short stories appropriate for adults and adolescents. The initial stories have a rather limited vocabulary, but they quickly become more challenging.

Reiff, T. *So Long, Snowman; The Family from Vietnam; A Time to Choose; Mollie's Year; Juan and Lucy; A Place for Everyone; The Shoplifting Game*. Belmont, Ca.: Fearon Pitman Publishers, Inc., 1979.

Seven very high-interest books based on 1,040 words, that make up the Lifeline Series. Students may not be interested in all seven books, but there is something here for everyone.

Hasinbiller, D.(Ed.). *Action*. New York: Scholastic Book Services, 1977.

A collection of twenty stories, most of which are appropriate for adolescents. Some stories, like "The Crate at Outpost 1," would be of very high interest to both adults and adolescents.

SUPPLEMENTAL READING FOR INSTRUCTORS

The instructor may find the following references useful. Be aware that while the authors frequently refer to children who are learning to read, the reading process applies to both adults and children.

Bond, Guy L.; Tinker, Miles A.; and Wasson, Barbara B. *Reading Difficulties* (4th ed.). Englewood Cliffs, N.J.: Prentice-Hall, Inc., 1979.

Ekwell, Eldon E. *Locating and Correcting Reading Difficulties* (2nd ed.). Columbus, Ohio: Charles E. Merrill Publishing Co., 1977.

Hall, Mary Ann. *Teaching Reading as a Language Experience*. Columbus, Ohio: Charles E. Merrill Publishing Co., 1970.

Hardin, Veralee B. and Pettit, Neila T. *A Guide to Ecological Screening and Assessment*. Dubuque, Iowa: William C. Brown Co., 1978.

Harris, Albert J., and Sipay, Edward R. *How to Increase Reading Ability* (6th ed.). New York: David McKay Co., Inc., 1975.

Ives, Josephine P.; Bursuk, Laura Z.; and Ives, Sumner A. *Word Identification Techniques*. Chicago: Rand McNally, 1979.

Kochevar, Deloise E. *Individualized Remedial Reading Techniques for the Classroom Teacher*. New York: Parker Publishing Co., Inc., 1975.

Kohl, Herbert. *Reading, How to*. New York: E. P. Dutton & Co., Inc., 1973.

Pope, Lillie. *Guidelines to Teaching Remedial Reading* (2nd ed.). New York: Book-Lab Inc., 1975.

Roswell, Florence and Natchez, Gladys. *Reading Disability: Diagnosis & Treatment* (2nd. ed.). New York: Basic Books, Inc., 1971.

Schubert, Delwyn and Torgerson, Theodor. *Improving the Reading Program* (4th ed.). Dubuque, Iowa: William C. Brown, Co., 1976.

Smith, Frank. *Understanding Reading*. New York: Holt, Rinehart & Winston, 1971.

Spache, George D. *Diagnosing & Correcting Reading Disabilities*. Boston: Allyn and Bacon Inc., 1976.

Spache, George D., and Spache, Evelyn B. *Reading in the Elementary School* (3rd ed.). Boston: Allyn & Bacon, Inc., 1973.

The Importance of Literacy Work

When eating out, have you ever considered the possibility that the person cooking your meal might not be able to read the poison warnings on a can of kitchen cleanser? When boarding an airplane, do you feel confident that all of the members of the ground crew can understand the repair manual? Are you aware of the likelihood that a number of soldiers who are responsible for making safety checks on our nation's military equipment may have trouble reading their instructions?

With the current statistics on the number of people who cannot read, these are not inappropriate questions. Although the statistics vary widely, the most conservative estimates suggest that at least 25 million people in the United States, or about 15 percent of the adult population, are functionally illiterate. A functional illiterate is generally defined as a person who can function only marginally in our society.

The functionally illiterate person cannot read the newspaper, cannot fill out an application for a job, cannot make sense of the deductions on her pay stub, and cannot fill out her income tax form. Indeed, it appears that the functionally illiterate person almost lives in another America. She cannot read the school notices that children bring home from school and cannot communicate in written form with her child's teachers. Cooking instructions on food products might as well be written in a foreign language. The functionally illiterate person cannot read restaurant menus, TV guides, or movie schedules. She cannot read the materials that will facilitate her being an informed, empowered citizen.

Even though we have partially outlined how the functionally illiterate cannot totally participate in our society, it is quite possible that some of those 25 million people work for your company, for the school your child attends, or for the city in which you live. No doubt, functional illiterates are heavily represented in the 8 million unemployed, but they also make up a substantial part of the work force. Twenty-five million people cannot be isolated.

While 25 million people cannot be isolated, they can be a drain on our nation's economy. Indirectly, the functionally illiterate put all of us at risk. As a nation, we are losing the intelligence and active participation of millions of people. The functionally illiterate are frequently underemployed since they are not employed in jobs where they can use all of their capabilities. Because they are frightened that change will expose their inability to read, they usually forgo on-the-job training and promotions. And, unfortunately, when reading is needed on their jobs, the functional illiterate can put all of us at risk. Functionally illiterate restaurant workers, ground crew workers, or servicemen who bluff their way through written directions may save their jobs, but they may hurt innocent people in the process.

The cost of illiteracy extends into areas that are harder to define. Think of the dread a parent experiences when she guesses at the instructions on her child's medicine or the fear a person experiences when she cannot look up an emergency number in the telephone directory. Think of how that same person feels when she leaves her neighborhood and cannot read the street signs. Think of the millions stuck in dead-end jobs and the countless numbers victimized because they cannot read. Then think of all the children who will not be read to or who will not receive any help with their schoolwork. If this problem is not addressed now, it will only multiply.

NOTE: To avoid sexist language, we have alternated male and female pronouns in this book. All references to instructors and students pertain to both sexes except when a specific person is being discussed.

If we are going to address this problem, we must recognize who the functional illiterate is. He is the man who always forgets to bring his reading glasses to work. She is the person who is always too busy to stop and read something. He is the person who brings forms home rather than filling them out at work. She is the one who gets her co-workers to explain things to her on the side, when other people are not around. He is the person with an excellent memory, who never refers to written notes. She is the person who says that she cannot understand your handwriting. He is the guy who carries a newspaper and pretends to read it. He or she very well may be your relative, your neighbor, or your best friend.

Rationale for New Beginnings in Reading

There are many different learning principles that have been used in developing *New Beginnings*. The discussion on the development of *New Beginnings* has been divided into two sections. The first section is an introduction to the general approaches to beginning reading. The second section, the rationale, deals with the cognitive and affective models and cites specific research. This second section is fairly technical in nature, so tread through it carefully.

A Layman's Overview of the Reading Process

New Beginnings is based on several accepted learning principles. It is generally recognized that repetition reinforces learning, that breaking a task into small units makes the task more manageable, and that students pay more attention to material that looks interesting. *New Beginnings* utilizes these principles by presenting only seven sight words per lesson and one phonics principle per book. The adult orientation and adult content provide interesting material for the adult to read.

While these general principles have been implemented, there is not a reading model that is universally accepted. Historically, there have been two basic theories as to how reading should be taught. The phonics approach emphasizes the sounds that the letters make. The contextual approach relies on the student's learning new words in the context of familiar sentences. Until 1964, an intense debate raged over which method was superior. In 1964 and 1965, the U.S. government funded a study to determine conclusively which method worked best.

While the study was extremely thorough, the results were not conclusive. The most important conclusion of the report was that students benefited from a combination of approaches, but it found that there was no superior approach for teaching reading. Unfortunately, the report left several questions unanswered, such as "Is one approach better or worse for a specific kind of student?" and "Is one type of method superior during any specific phase of learning to read?"

Although this study left some questions unanswered, most publishing companies responded by including both the phonics and contextual approaches in their reading programs. At the same time, reading theorists also redefined their old concepts according to cognitive psychology, and a third model emerged.

Those who had supported the contextual approach to reading now see the student as coming to the written page with a strong idea as to what he will find there. They do not see the student focusing on individual letters or words, but rather they believe that the student uses minimal graphic clues while projecting meaning onto the page. They believe that the student uses context rather than phonics to read unknown words.

The phonics-oriented theorists maintain that the student's mind is like a blank slate and that he can derive meaning only by looking at the letters.

In addition, a third reading model has developed. This model states that a reader will alternate between using context and using phonics, depending on the reading situation and the reader's ability. This model effectively explains much of the research that has been done with beginning readers, and *New Beginnings* is based on this model. Students who use *New Beginnings* are taught how to use both context and phonics.

Although finding an appropriate reading model was important in the development of *New Beginnings*, it is not based solely on reading principles. Research on the relationship between learning and the student's self-concept was also utilized. Theorists in this area

NOTE: To avoid sexist language, we have alternated male and female pronouns in this book. All references to instructors and students pertain to both sexes except when a specific person is being discussed.

suggest that reading material should be success-oriented. *New Beginnings* provides for success by providing large amounts of repetition and small skill increments. In addition, the exercises were developed on the premise that the student is or can become an active, competent partner in the learning process.

Theoretical Rationale for New Beginnings in Reading

There are numerous questions that must be addressed in the development of reading materials. Some questions generated by this series include: How should sight words be presented? How many words should be presented in each lesson? What types of words are easiest for the beginning reader to learn? What are the advantages and disadvantages of presenting words in isolation or in context? Should pictures be used as cues? Should phonics be taught? Should word families be presented? How important is the use of high-interest material? What materials interest adult beginning readers? How much repetition should be provided? Obviously, the list could be extended.

While the creation of appropriate questions is important to the development of a program, it is only the first step. Eventually, questions have to be answered, and answers must be implemented in usable, affordable materials.

In answering such questions, a person can try several routes. Initially, he or she may fall back upon such traditional "truths" as "repetition is good," "high-interest material is important," and "the fewer words presented, the more likely it is that they will be mastered." While dependence upon basic "truths" may simplify a rationale, the limited number of acknowledged truths leaves most of the questions unanswered.

An author might then take these unanswered questions to the research literature. At that point, the author would realize that research results are not usually applicable to instructional design. Venezy (1977) has suggested that most research focuses on subjects for only ten to fifteen minutes, in situations that are dissimilar to those actually experienced by students. While generalizing the results of such studies to fit the classroom is suspect at best, the overabundance of experimental conditions frequently ends up with conflicting results.

An industrious person might then study various reading models that attempt to explain the conflicting data. Even with the best model for explaining contradictory results, it becomes apparent that there is no "best" model for instructional design. Most models explain the reading behaviors of mature readers. No model has delineated a sequence of stages from immature to mature reading (Venezy, 1977). To complicate the process even further, no model even mentions adult beginning readers.

Cognitive Models

Historically, there have been two major cognitive models which attempt to explain how reading occurs; the "top-down" model and the "bottom-up" model.

TOP-DOWN MODELS

Although the specifics proposed by individual theorists may vary, the top-down model basically hypothesizes that the mature reader relies extensively on use of context and the repetition of certain spellings. In his article "Reading: A Psycholinguistic Guessing Game," Goodman (1976) describes reading as just that—a guessing game. He goes on to say that reading is "a selective process. It involves partial use of available minimal language cues selected from perceptual input on the basis of the reader's expectations. As this partial information is processed, tentative decisions are made to be confirmed, rejected, or refined as reading progresses" (pg. 498).

Through an analysis of miscues, Goodman has arrived at the conclusion that "as a child develops reading skill and speed, he uses fewer graphic cues" (pg. 504). Goodman believes that the reader reconstructs the writer's meaning by "monitoring his choices" (pg. 483). This emphasis upon what the reader brings to the text has resulted in the labeling of Goodman's theory (and others like it) as being top-down.

BOTTOM-UP MODELS

In contrast to the top-down theorists, researchers who propose bottom-up models suggest that reading is a serial process involving word perceptions. Gough (1976) adamantly states that "the reader is not a guesser" (pg. 532). He hypothesizes that the reader "plods through the sentence, letter by letter, and word by word" (pg. 532). While Gough's letter-by-letter analysis represents an extreme bottom-up framework, others (LaBerge and Samuels, 1976) suggest that decoding shifts from letters to syllables, syllables to words, and finally, words to clusters of words.

Although their specific orientations may vary, bottom-up theorists can be represented as those who perceive reading as text-oriented. The concept of automaticity, defined as a skill that can be completed while attention is directed elsewhere or the ability to do two things at one time, is one experimental model the bottom-up theorists emphasize in their research.

INTERACTIVE MODELS

As neither the top-down nor the bottom-up theorists have attempted to account for the data accumulated by the other group, each group leaves important questions unanswered. A key top-down hypothesis that emphasizes the mature readers' reliance upon context for reading has been called into question by numerous studies (Stanovich, 1980). Researchers have also suggested that the hypothesis-testing theory proposed by proponents of top-down models is not reasonable in terms of the processing time that is actually available to the reader (McConkie and Rayner, 1976; Samuels, Dahl and Archwamety, 1974; Wildman and Kling, 1978-1979). The bottom-up model has also been criticized because it does not take into account how context facilitates the beginning reader's readings.

In an attempt to resolve seemingly paradoxical evidence that both supports and refutes bottom-up and top-down models, Rumelhart (1977) has proposed an interactive model. Essentially, he suggests that bottom-up and top-down processes both direct and constrain each other. Stanovich has extended Rumelhart's interactive model with a compensatory component. He hypothesizes that when one process is deficient, the other can compensate for that deficiency. The reading behaviors explained by Stanovich's model include not only findings that poor readers rely more heavily on context for decoding than do good readers, but also data that indicates that good readers resort to the use of context when their decoding is experimentally slowed.

The interactive-compensatory model proposed by Stanovich (1980) has been selected as an appropriate model for *New Beginnings in Reading* for several reasons. It explains contradictory data in a sensible way. It acknowledges the relative strengths and weaknesses of top-down and bottom-up processing for readers at various stages of development. It is appealing at a "gut level" because it meshes with the basic remedial reading technique of building upon the student's strengths, while remediating his or her weak areas.

Specific Research

Biemiller (1970) observed first-grade children's reading errors over a period of seven months and concluded that proficiency developed as students moved from reliance on context to reliance on contextual and graphic cues. Similarly, Weber (1970) and Biemiller (1979) noted that better first-grade readers were more attentive to graphic cues than were poor readers. While the importance of teaching phonics can be inferred from both the Weber and the Biemiller studies, other research has demonstrated the importance of teaching adult beginning readers to read for meaning.

In a seminal, ethnographic study of the word recognition strategies of adult beginning readers, Boraks and Schumacher (1981) noted that "few adult beginning readers made much use of semantic cues" (pg. 22). However, they went on to say that "it appeared that adult beginning readers who used strategies associated with success were more aware of the fact that they had to understand what they read" (pg. 25). Specific instructional guidelines recommended by Boraks and Schumacher include teaching students "to monitor meaning, make successive attempts, manipulate the vowel, and use syllables" (pg. 25).

Teaching students a variety of strategies has not been identified as a problem in any of the research literature. McNeil and Donant (1980) significantly improved 90 second-, third-, and fourth-graders' ability to use context, phonics, and word analysis in decoding unfamiliar words by exposing them to three training sessions on each of the methods.

Paralleling this research on the advantages of teaching both phonics and context, Ehri and Roberts (1979) and Ehri and Wilce (1980) reported that various benefits occur when words are taught in isolation and in context. Meanwhile, Entwistle (1971) has noted the importance of presenting words with multiple meanings through multiple contexts.

Affective Models

Zajonc (1980) has suggested that a complex interrelationship exists between the cognitive and affective factors. This is what Piaget refers to as the "two banks of the same river." The remainder of this rationale will address the affective models as they relate to adult beginning readers.

In 1941, Gates reviewed the existing literature on

personality maladjustment and reading disorders and came to the conclusion that "personality maladjustment is frequently found to coexist with reading disability. The more serious the reading retardation, the greater is the probability that maladjustment also exists " (pg. 82-83). The "numerous forms" of maladjustment listed by Gates include symptoms frequently observed by instructors of adult beginning readers: nervousness, withdrawal, defeatism, and chronic worry. At that time, Gates suggested clinical insight combined with skillful general management as a means of reorienting the student to successful learning.

In redefining metacognition as containing or coexisting with affective components, Athey (1981) has presented a promising framework for understanding the complex interaction between affective factors and severe reading disabilities. She has suggested that the kind, quality, and number of statements a student makes to himself regarding such areas as the perceived difficulty to materials, assessment of his own ability to read the materials, and his interest in and value assigned to materials may differentiate good readers from poor ones. While Athey raises many provocative questions about the relationship of reading achievement to self-concept, independence, and values, she has left it to others to speculate on how the instructor might influence the student's self-concept, independence, values, and statements made to himself about them.

Belz (1983) has described an approach that combines basic skills instruction with psychotherapeutic techniques. According to Belz, "failure-ridden encounters with instruction" can be restructured into interactions that are more functional by "helping individuals understand how poor academic self-concept has interfered with their ability to achieve in situations involving educational tasks" (pg. 3). As students experience success in learning tasks, they begin to redefine themselves as learners. While this model emphasizes the instructor's role in helping students attribute success to personal effort, success-oriented materials do play a basic role.

Working within a social psychology framework, Coles (1983) comes to conclusions similar to those offered by Belz and Athey. He suggests that "the change from illiteracy to literacy must include a transformation of self-concept" (pg. 10). Through a case study, he details both the instructor's role in helping students redefine themselves as learners and the importance of using materials that aid students in overcoming their feelings of stupidity.

Not surprisingly, Gates, Athey, Belz, and Coles all emphasize the same basic point: the remedial reading student's instructional needs are not limited to the cognitive domain. The directives from these affective theorists are clear cut—beginning reading materials should be success-oriented. The content of beginning reading materials should reflect the author's and instructor's belief that the adult beginning reader is intellectually competent. Issues important to adults, as well as those addressing the beginning reader's concerns, should be used for teaching the basic skills. The process of learning to read should be presented in such a way that the student is seen as an active, competent partner in the learning process.

REFERENCES

Athey, I. Reading: The affective domain reconceptualized. In B. Hutson (Ed.), *Advances in reading/language research*. Greenwich, Conn.: JAI Press, 1981.

Belz, E. *The process of adult educational therapy*. Unpublished paper, College of Medicine and Dentistry of New Jersey, Piscataway, 1983.

Biemiller, A. The development of the use of graphic and contextual information as children learn to read. *Reading Research Quarterly*, 1970, 6, 75–96.

Biemiller, A. Changes in the use of graphic and contextual information as functions of passage difficulty and reading achievement level. *Journal of Reading Behavior*, 1979, 11, 307–318.

Boraks, N., and Schumacher, S. *Ethnographic research on word recognition strategies of adult beginning readers: Summary report*. Richmond: School of Education, Virginia Commonwealth University, 1981.

Coles, G. *Adult illiteracy and learning theory: A study of cognition and activity*. Unpublished paper, College of Medicine and Dentistry of New Jersey, Piscataway, 1983.

Ehri, L. C., and Roberts, K. T. Do beginners learn printed words better in context or in isolation? *Child Development*, 1979, 50, 675–685.

Ehri, L. C., and Wilce, L. S. Do beginners learn to read function words better in sentences or in lists? *Reading Research Quarterly*, 1980, 15, 451–476.

Entwistle, D. Implications of language socialization for reading models and learning to read. In F. Davis (Ed.), *The literature of research in reading with emphasis on models*. New Brunswick, N.J.: Graduate School of Education, Rutgers, 1971.

Gates, A. I. The role of personality maladjustment in reading disability. *Journal of Genetic Psychology*, 1941, 59, 77–83.

Goodman, K. Reading: A psycholinguistic guessing game. In H. Singer & R. Ruddell (Eds.), *Theoretical models and processes of reading* (2nd ed.). Newark, Del.: International Reading Association, 1976.

Gough, P. B. One second of reading. In H. Singer and R. Ruddell (Eds.), *Theoretical models and processes of reading* (2nd ed.). Newark, Del.: International Reading Association, 1976.

LaBerge, D., and Samuels, S. J. Toward a theory of automatic information processing in reading. In H. Singer and R. Ruddell (Eds.), *Theoretical models and processes of reading* (2nd ed.) Newark, Del.: International Reading Association, 1976.

McConkie, G. W., and Rayner, K. Identifying the span of the effective stimulus in reading: Literature review and theories of reading. In H. Singer and R. Ruddell (Eds.), *Theoretical models and processes of reading* (2nd ed.). Newark, Del.: International Reading Association, 1976.

McNeil, J. D., and Donant, L. Transfer effect of word recognition strategies. *Journal of Reading Behavior*, 1980, 12, 97–103.

Rumelhart, D. Toward an interactive model of reading. In S. Dornic (Ed.), *Attention and performance*, VI. Hillsdale, N.J.: Erlbaum Associates, 1977.

Samuels, S. J., Dahl, P., and Archwamety, T. Effect of hypothesis/test training on reading skill. *Journal of Educational Psychology*, 1974, 66, 835–844.

Singer, H., Samuels, S. J., and Spiroff, J. The effects of pictures and contextual conditions on learning responses to printed words. *Reading Research Quarterly*, 1973/1974, 9, 555–567.

Stanovich, K. Toward an interactive-compensatory model of individual differences in the development of reading fluency. *Reading Research Quarterly*, 1980, 15, 32–71.

Venezy, R. I. Research on reading processes: A historical perspective. *American Psychologist*, 1977, 32, 339–345.

Weber, R. M. First graders' use of grammatical context in reading In H. Levin and J. Williams (Eds.), *Basic studies in reading*. New York: Basic Books, 1970.

Wildman, D. M., and Kling, M. Semantic, syntactic, and spatial anticipation in reading. *Reading Research Quarterly*, 1978/1979, 14, 128–164.

Zajorc, R. B. Feeling and thinking. *American Psychologist*, 1980, 35, 151–175.

CONTEMPORARY BOOKS, INC.
ADULT EDUCATION
DEPARTMENT D2
ATTENTION: WENDY HARRIS
180 NORTH MICHIGAN AVENUE
CHICAGO, ILLINOIS 60601

BILL TO _____

ATTENTION _____

ADDRESS _____

CITY _____ STATE _____ ZIP _____

PURCHASE ORDER NO. _____

DATE _____

SHIP TO _____

ATTENTION _____

ADDRESS _____

CITY _____ STATE _____ ZIP _____

BUYER _____

PHONE NUMBER _____

QUAN.	TITLE NO.	TITLE	INSTITUTIONAL NET PRICE
		NEW BEGINNINGS IN READING	
	5195-7	Placement Test (1)	1.50
	5061-6	Placement Test Set (5)	6.75
	5177-9	Groundbreaker Exercises	3.50
	5176-0	Book 1	3.50
	5175-2	Book 2	3.50
	5174-4	Book 3	3.50
	5173-6	Book 4	3.50
	5172-8	Book 5	3.50
	5170-1	Book 6	3.50
	5169-8	Book 7	3.50
	5167-1	Book 8	3.50
	5166-3	Instructor's Guide	3.50

Net prices subject to change without notice. The net prices quoted on this form are exclusive of freight costs, which will be prepaid and added to your invoice. The net prices represent our prices to institutional customers and are not intended to control the resale price. All terms net 30 days F.O.B. Chicago.